RECORDED VERSIONS GUITAR

AUTHENTIC TRANSCRIPTIONS
WITH NOTES AND TABLATURE

# VINTAGE ROCK

W9-BIG-932

ISBN 0-634-01557-5

HAL•LEONARD
CORPORATION

7777 W. BLUEMOUND RD. P.O. BOX 13819 MILWAUKEE, WI 53213

Visit Hal Leonard Online at
**www.halleonard.com**

# VINTAGE ROCK

# INTRODUCTION

The glorious explosion of rock in the sixties and seventies reflected the sum total of nearly fifty years of American popular music. Blues, from the solo acoustic Delta numbers in the late twenties to the stomping, electrified Chicago boogies twenty years later and its offshoots R&B and soul, always had the most pervasive influence. Almost concurrently, country music was developing an idiosyncratic approach to I, IV, and V chords. Pop and Tin Pan Alley music from the thirties and forties would supply lyric themes and emphasis on I-vi-ii-V chord progressions. Jazz, particularly the swing variety exemplified by Count Basie circa World War II, contributed the "big beat" that encouraged exuberant dancing. Elements of all the genres coalesced in the early fifties to create rock 'n' roll, fueled by the new and innovative solidbody electric guitar.

The first wave of postwar baby boomers were going through their adolescence in the late fifties, digging the raw energy of Chuck Berry, Little Richard, Jerry Lee Lewis, and the early Elvis. Some were inspired to play by two seminal guitar heroes, Buddy Holly and Duane Eddy, but cosmic forces were at work that would ignite a mass cultural and musical revolution. On November 23, 1963, President John F. Kennedy was assassinated in Dallas, Texas, destroying the veil of secure innocence and the unbridled optimism engendered by the young, virile leader of the free world. Then, shortly after the New Year, while the country was still in mourning, four brash, long haired English rock 'n' rollers appeared on the Ed Sullivan TV show. Their music, via "I Want to Hold Your Hand," and word of the phenomenon they were creating in their wake in Europe had already whetted young appetites starved for a distraction. The Beatles, followed by the Rolling Stones and their marauding fellow countrymen in what would be known as the British Invasion, turned "rock 'n' roll" into "rock," reinventing the genre and imbuing it with a power and potential heretofore unrealized. The bands that followed from the U.S.A., especially the West Coast, and from the British Isles, would also incorporate aspects of folk, classical, and Near Eastern music in a delirious frenzy of boundless experimentation.

A comprehensive selection of '60s and '70s classics is presented in the following pages. Blues-based rock swaggers and struts in the music of quite a few powerful units. Cream's "White Room" shows Eric Clapton riffing like one of the "Kings" of the blues while romping on a wah-wah pedal. Big Leslie West from Mountain pays homage to "Slowhand" as he squeezes a squalling, squealing tone from his Les Paul Junior on the thumping "Mississippi Queen." Real Southern rockers Lynyrd Skynyrd swing with the jazz standard "Call Me the Breeze" and the triple-axe attack of Allen Collins, Gary Rossington, and Steve Gaines. Bringing boogie to English glam rock, T. Rex's Marc Bolan chugs away on "Bang a Gong (Get It On)." The Guess Who from Canada take a pot shot at United States womanhood and politics as Randy Bachman sustains with the tonality of a clarinet on "American Woman." Bachman strikes his Gretsch again with the good humor of "Takin' Care of Business" by Bachman-Turner Overdrive. Rick Derringer wrote the rollicking "Rock and Roll Hoochie Koo" for his buddy Johnny Winter and then went and cut the definitive version himself. Last but not least, the Rolling Stones show why they have compiled the most impressive "record" of blues-rock with the intertwined guitars of Keith Richards and Mick Taylor on "Tumblin' Dice" from the epochal *Exile on Main Street.*

Heavy riff rock with a tangential relationship to the blues is purveyed by Deep Purple and Ritchie Blackmore on the smokey "Woman from Tokyo." Donald "Buck Dharma" Roeser from the menacing Blue Öyster Cult wreaks havoc on the thunderous "Godzilla." One of the lesser-known groups from the seventies who blazed briefly was Nazareth with Manny Charlton leading his Scottish lads on the thunderous "Hair of the Dog."

The spirit, if not the form of the blues, is much in evidence on the Jimi Hendrix version of "Hey Joe." The same could be said for Pink Floyd's shuffling "Money," highlighted by David Gilmour's soaring Strat. "Free Ride" by the Edgar Winter Group features the twin guitars of Floyd Radford and Ronnie Montrose and a hook that owes more than a slight debt to the chordal embellishments developed by Hendrix. Holland's Golden Earring conjure a spooky, atmospheric "road song" with the stripped-down shuffle rhythm of "Radar Love" and George Kooyman's snakey leads. While penned by Broadway's Jerry Ragovoy, Janis Joplin's version of "Piece of My Heart" oozes bluesy soul and is complemented by the San Francisco psychedelia of Sam Andrew and James Gurley.

Classical music exerts a noticeable influence on the Beatles' stately "Let It Be," with Paul McCartney on piano and George Harrison on lead guitar, and Aerosmith's epic power ballad "Dream On," driven by Joe Perry and Brad Whitford. Operatic would certainly be a better description for Meatloaf's "Two Out of Three Ain't Bad" with producer Todd Rundgren providing stellar six-string support. "Jesus Is Just Alright With Me" by the Doobie Brothers is the lone offering that betrays its folk roots with Tom Johnston and Patrick Simmons weaving a surging wall of rhythm.

—Dave Rubin

# American Woman

**Written by Burton Cummings, Randy Bachman,
Gary Peterson and Jim Kale**

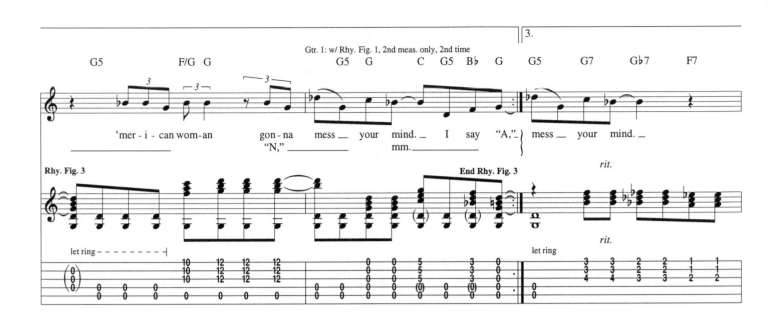

'mer - i - can wom-an gon - na mess _ your mind. _ I say "A," mess your mind. _
"N," _ mm.

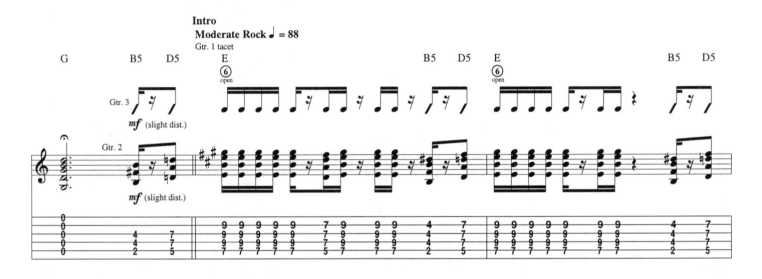

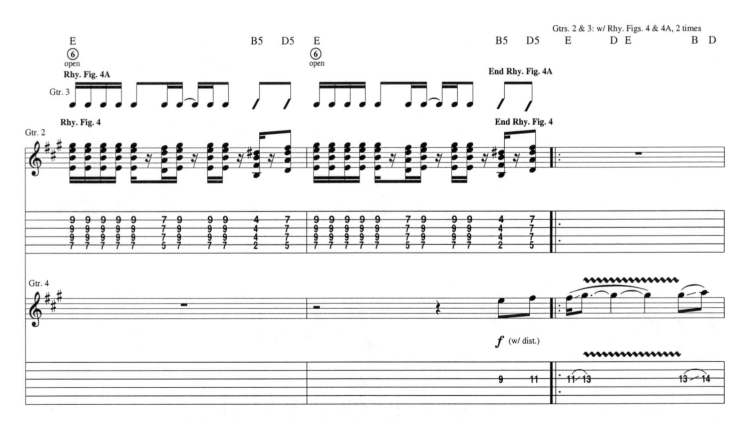

Gtr. 4: w/ Fill 1, 1st time
Gtr. 4: w/ Fill 3, 2nd time

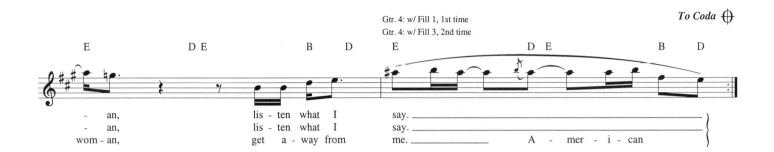

- an,        lis - ten what I      say. _____
- an,        lis - ten what I      say. _____
wom - an,     get   a - way from   me. _____ A - mer - i - can

### Guitar Solo
Gtrs. 2 & 3: w/ Rhy. Figs. 4 & 4A, 8 times, simile

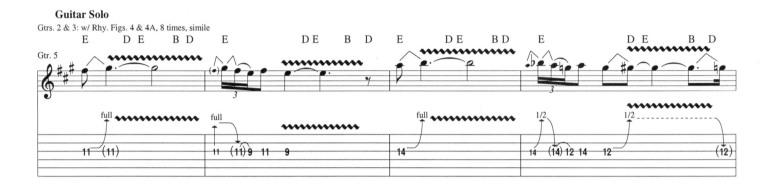

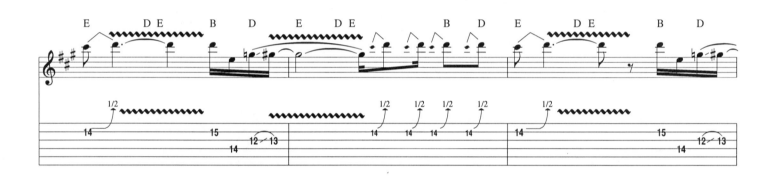

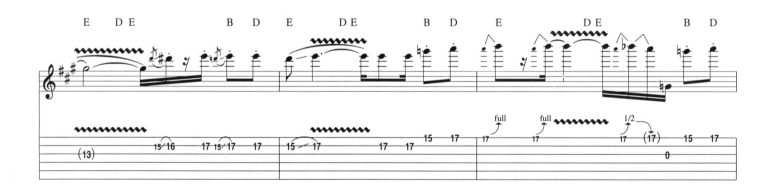

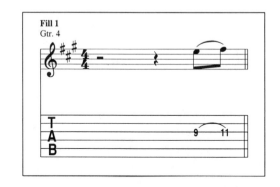

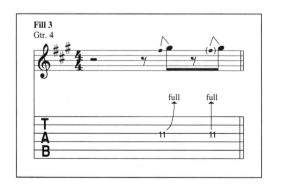

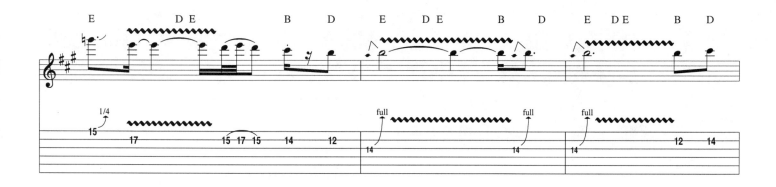

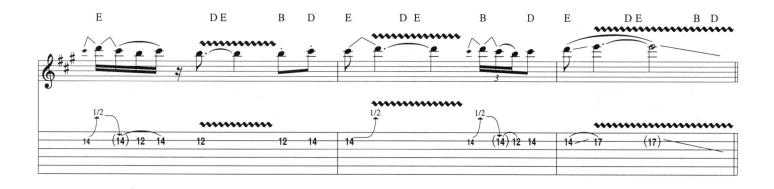

**Interlude**
Gtr. 4 tacet

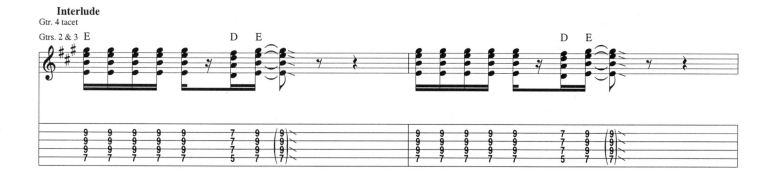

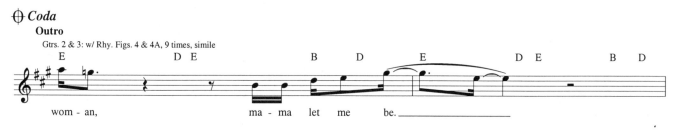

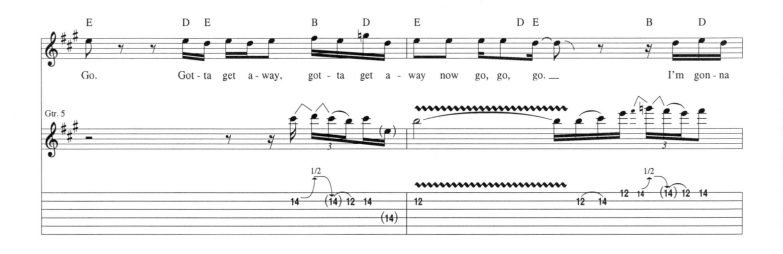

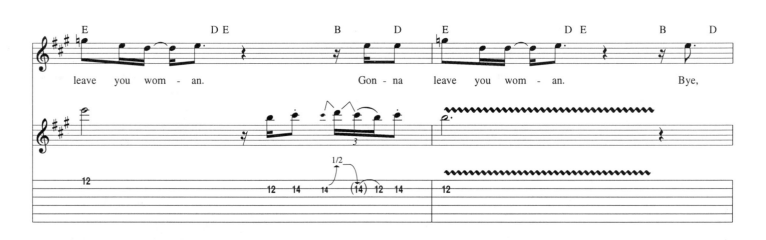

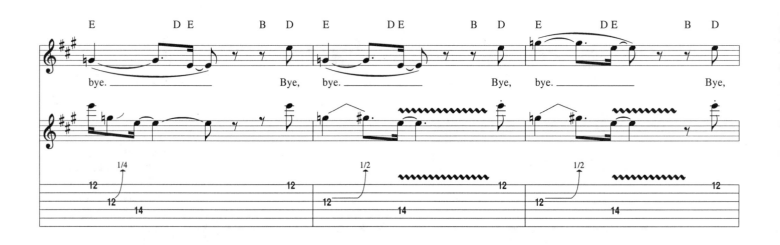

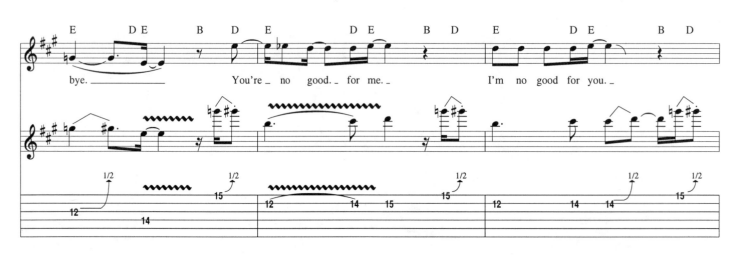

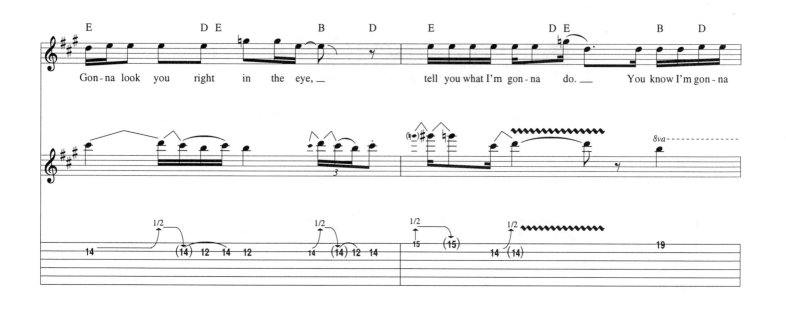

Gon - na look you right in the eye, __ tell you what I'm gon - na do. __ You know I'm gon - na

leave. You know I'm gon - na go. You know I'm gon - na

Fade Out

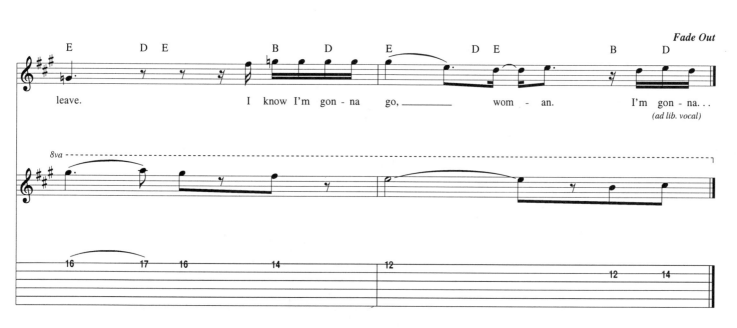

leave. I know I'm gon - na go, _____ wom - an. I'm gon - na...

*(ad lib. vocal)*

# Bang a Gong (Get It On)

**Words and Music by Marc Bolan**

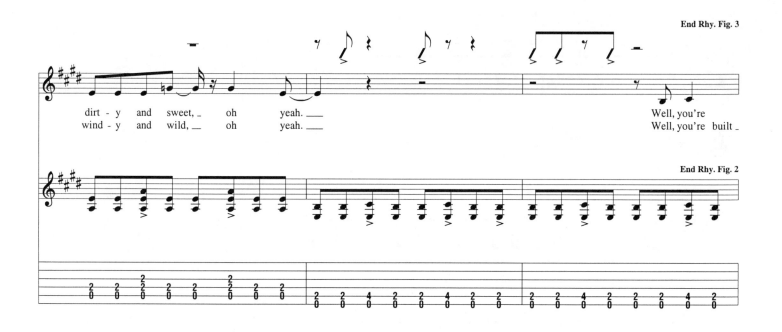

dirt - y and sweet,__ oh yeah.__ Well, you're
wind - y and wild,__ oh yeah.__ Well, you're built__

End Rhy. Fig. 2

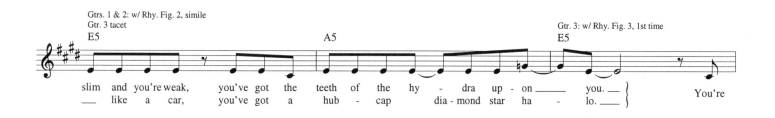

Gtrs. 1 & 2: w/ Rhy. Fig. 2, simile
Gtr. 3 tacet

Gtr. 3: w/ Rhy. Fig. 3, 1st time

E5                                      A5                              E5

slim and you're weak, you've got the teeth of the hy - dra up - on __ you. __ You're

Gtr. 3: w/ Rhy. Fig. 3, last two meas., 2nd time

A5                              E5

dirt - y, sweet and you're my girl. ____ Get it on. __

**Chorus**

G5                      A5                      E5/B

Rhy. Fig. 4A
Gtr. 3

____ Bang a gong. __ Get it on. Get it on. __

Gtrs. 1 & 2
Rhy. Fig. 4

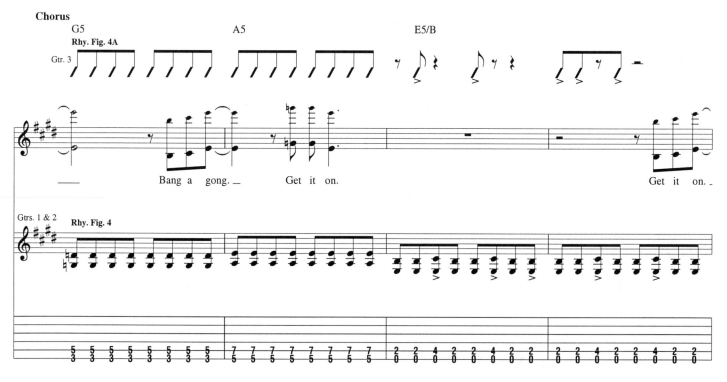

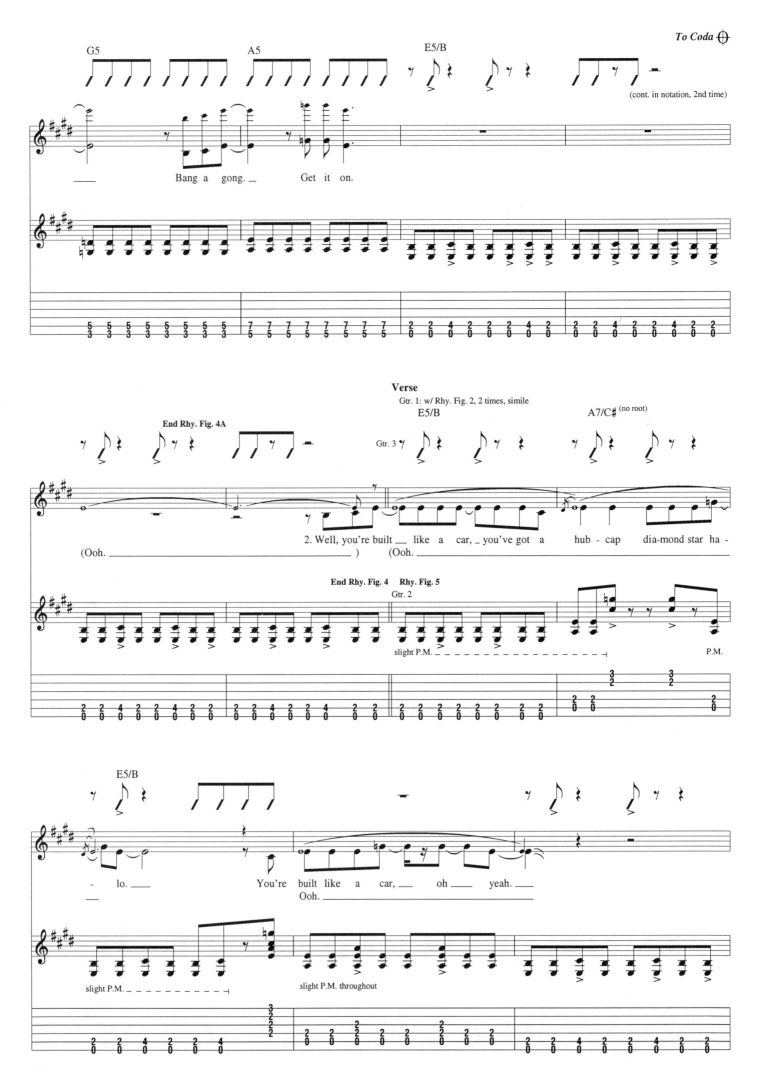

(cont. in notation, 2nd time)

Bang a gong. Get it on.

**Verse**
Gtr. 1: w/ Rhy. Fig. 2, 2 times, simile

End Rhy. Fig. 4A

2. Well, you're built __ like a car, __ you've got a hub-cap dia-mond star ha-
(Ooh. _____ ) (Ooh. _____

End Rhy. Fig. 4   Rhy. Fig. 5
Gtr. 2

slight P.M.                                        P.M.

- lo. ___   You're built like a car, __ oh __ yeah. __
   ___      Ooh. __

slight P.M.          slight P.M. throughout

# Call Me the Breeze

**Words and Music by John Cale**

* Chord symbols reflect basic tonality.

**Verse**

1. Call me the breeze; __ I keep blow - in' down __ the road. __

__ Well, now, they

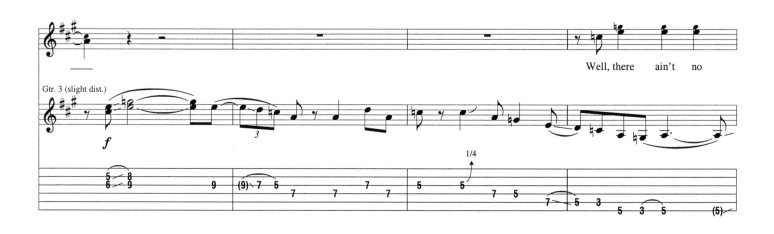

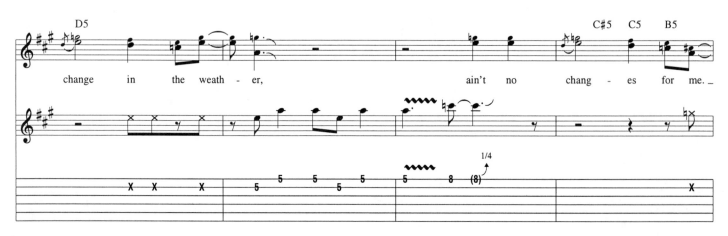

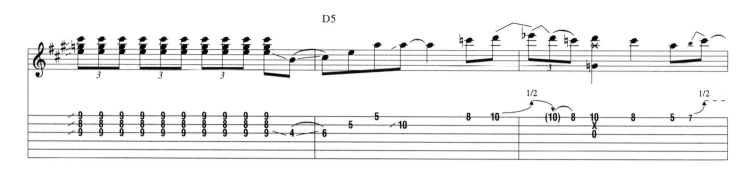

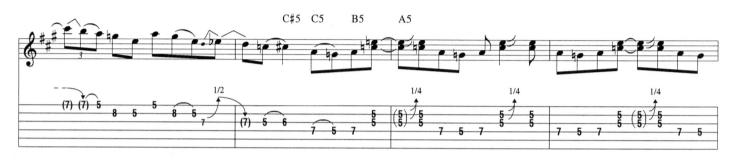

**Verse**

Gtrs. 1 & 2: w/ Rhy. Figs. 1 & 1A, simile  Gtr. 4 tacet

3. Well, I got that green light,_ ba - by;

I got to keep mov - in' on. ___

Well, I got that green light, __ babe; __

I got to keep mov - in' on. ___

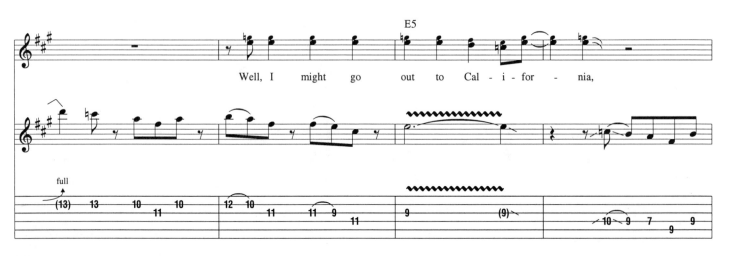

Well, I might go out to Cal - i - for - nia,

might go down to Geor - gia, I don't know. _____

**Piano Solo**

Gtrs. 1 & 2: w/ Rhy. Fig. 1A, simile

Gtr. 3 tacet

string noise

Gtrs. 1 & 2: w/ Rhy. Fig. 1A, simile

Gtr. 3

4. Well, I

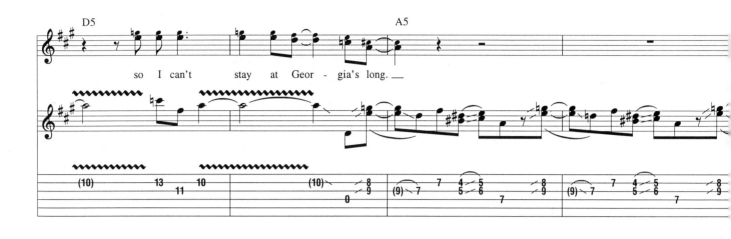

so I can't stay at Geor - gia's long. _

**Verse**

Gtrs. 1 & 2: w/ Rhy. Figs. 1 & 1A, 1st 20 meas., simile

5. Well, now, they call me the breeze; _

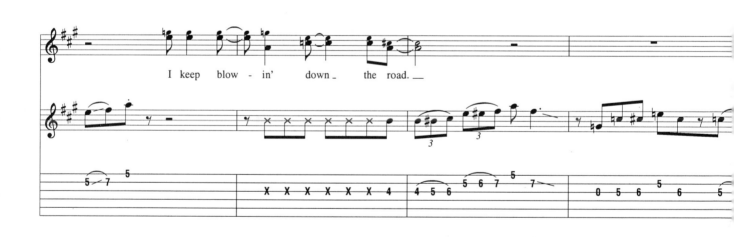

I keep blow - in' down _ the road. _

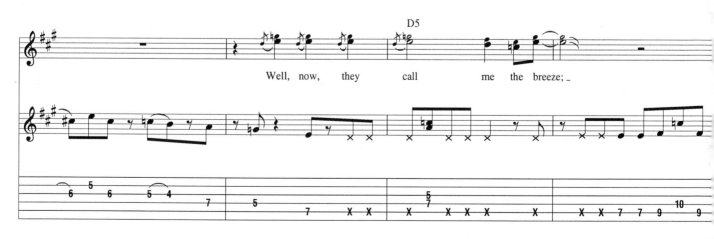

Well, now, they call me the breeze; _

# Dream On

**Words and Music by Steven Tyler**

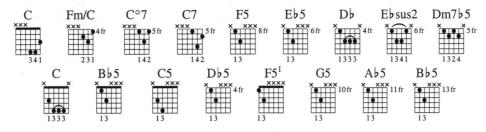

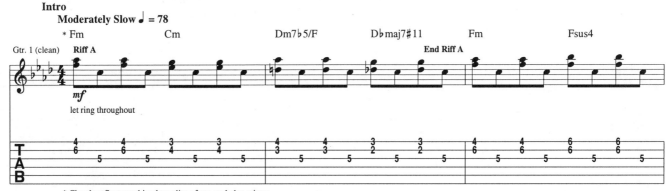

**Intro**

**Moderately Slow** ♩ = 78

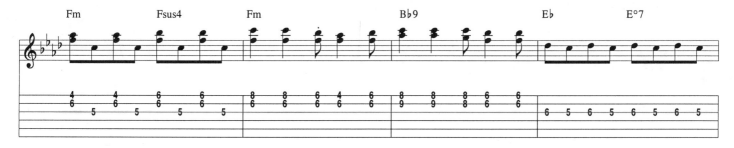

\* Chords reflect combined tonality of gtr. and elec. piano.

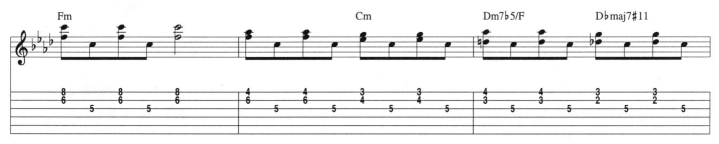

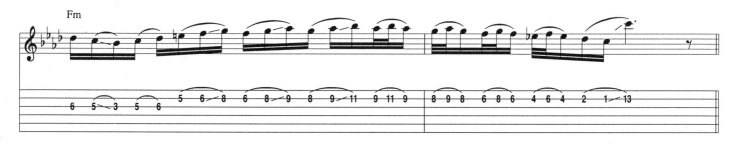

1. Ev-'ry time ___ that I look in the mir - ror, all these lines ___ in my face get-tin' clear - er.

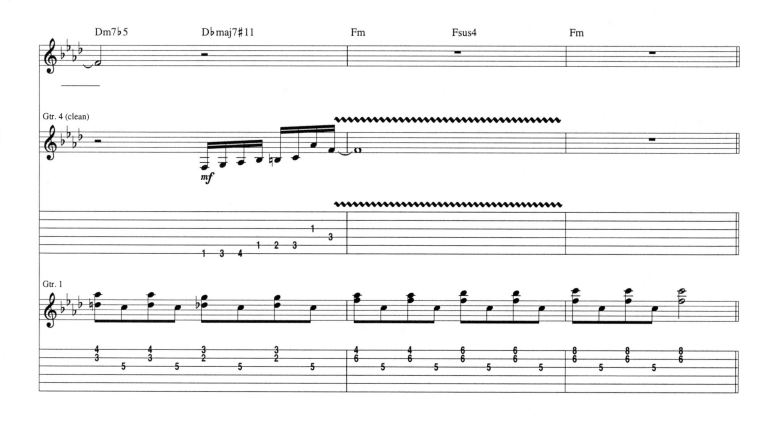

**Verse**

Gtr. 4 tacet
Gtr. 1: w/ Riff A, 4 times

2. Half _ my life's in book's writ-ten pa - ges, lived and learned from fools and from sag - es.

You know _ it's true _____ all these things _____ come back to you. _____

**𝄋 Pre-Chorus**

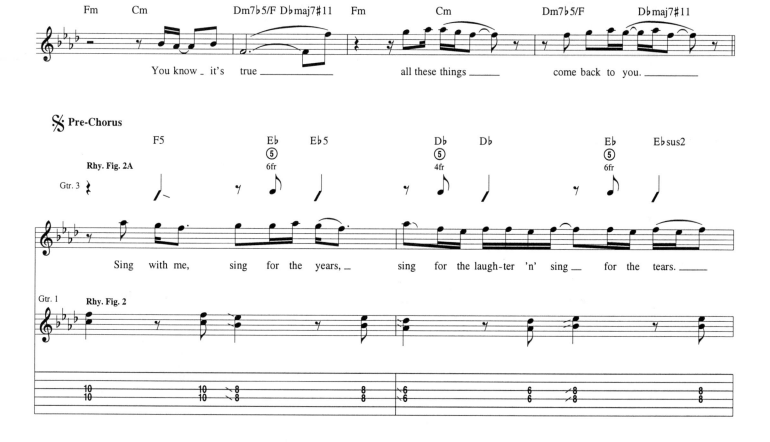

Sing with me, sing for the years, _ sing for the laugh-ter 'n' sing _ for the tears. _____

Sing _ with me if it's just for to - day, _ may-be to - mor - row the good Lord will take you a - way. _

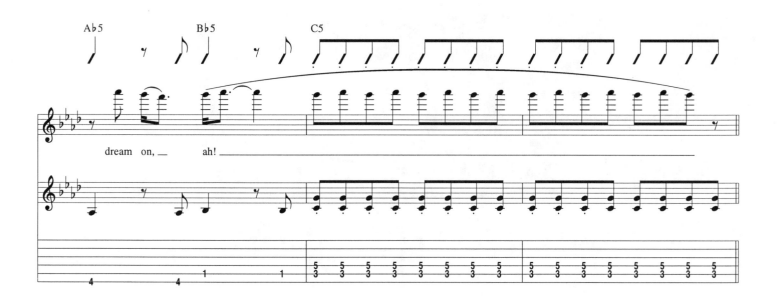

dream on, — ah! _____

### Pre-Chorus

Gtrs. 1 & 3: w/ Rhy. Figs. 1 & 1A

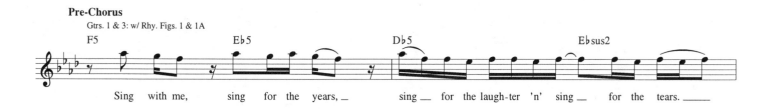

F5          Eb5          Db5          Ebsus2

Sing with me, sing for the years, — sing — for the laugh-ter 'n' sing — for the tears. _____

F5          Eb5          Db5          Ebsus2

Sing it with me if it's just for to - day, — may-be to - mor - row the good Lord will take you a-way.

Gtrs. 1 & 3: w/ Rhy. Figs. 2 & 2A

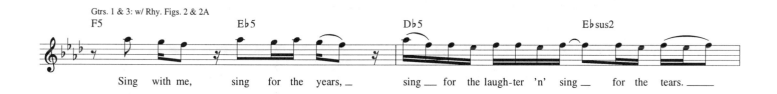

F5          Eb5          Db5          Ebsus2

Sing with me, sing for the years, — sing — for the laugh-ter 'n' sing — for the tears. _____

Gtr. 4: w/ Riff B

F5          Eb5          Dm7b5          Db          C

Sing it with me if it's just for to - day, — may-be to - mor-row the good Lord will take you a - way. _

### Outro

Gtrs. 1, 3 & 4 tacet

*Repeat and Fade*

Gtr. 2

N.C.(C5)

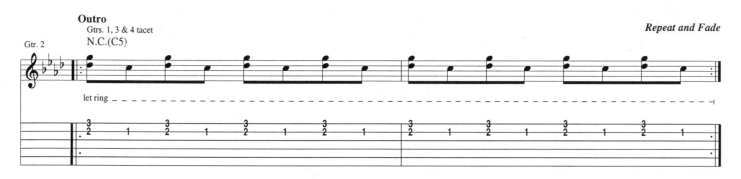

let ring _ _ _ _ _ _ _ _ _ _ _ _

# Free Ride

## By Dan Hartman

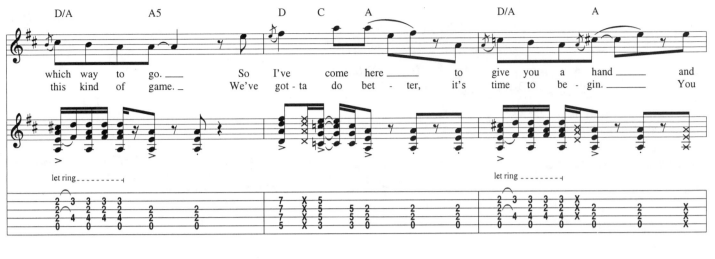

which way to go. ___ So I've come here ___ to give you a hand ___ and
this kind of game. ___ We've got-ta do bet-ter, it's time to be-gin. ___ You

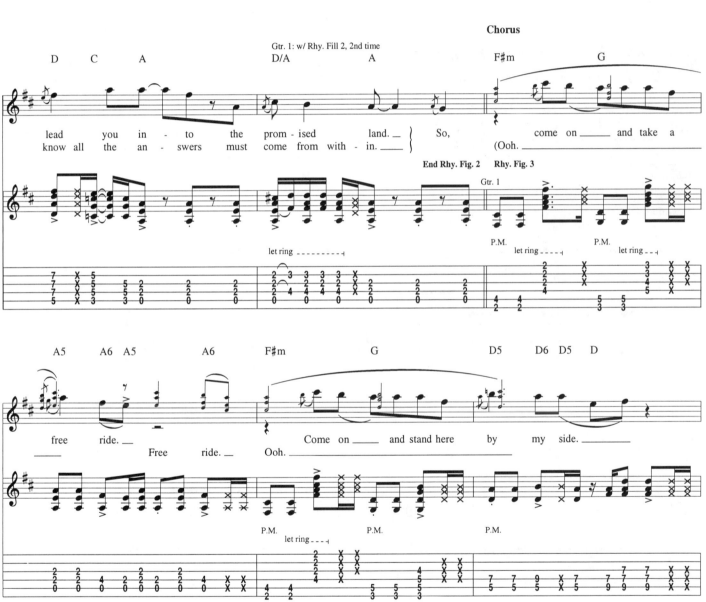

**Chorus**

lead you in - to the prom - ised land. ___ So, come on ___ and take a
know all the an - swers must come from with - in. ___ (Ooh. ___

free ride. ___ Free ride. ___ Ooh. ___ Come on ___ and stand here by my side. ___

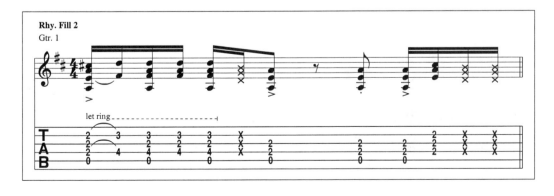

**Rhy. Fill 2**
Gtr. 1

Come on ____ and take a free ride.

Ooh. _____ )

*Two gtrs. arr. for one.

## Guitar Solo

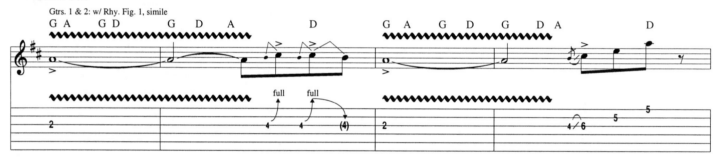

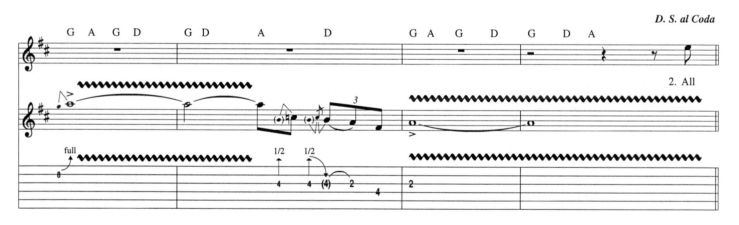

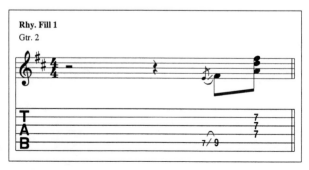

*Coda*

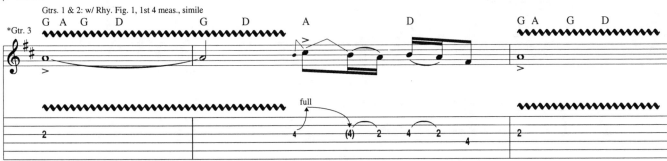

*Two gtrs. arr. for one.

**Guitar Solo**

Gtr. 1: w/ Rhy. Fig. 2, simile
Gtr. 2 tacet

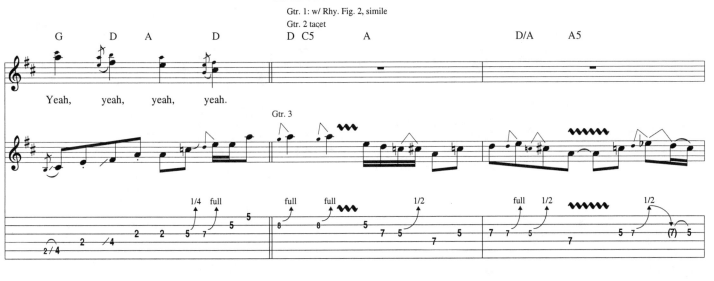

Yeah,      yeah,      yeah,      yeah.

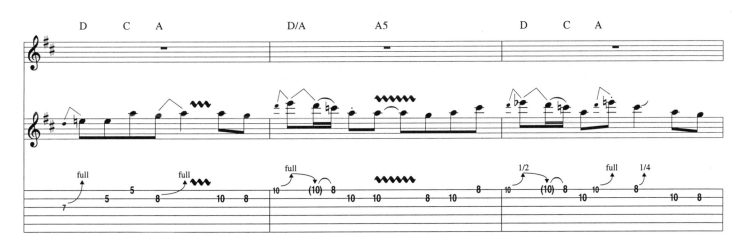

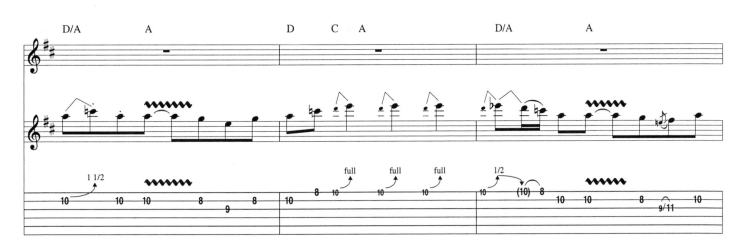

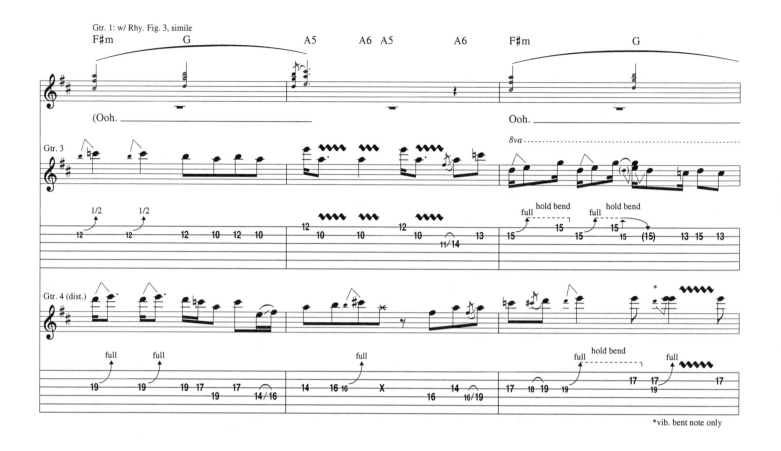

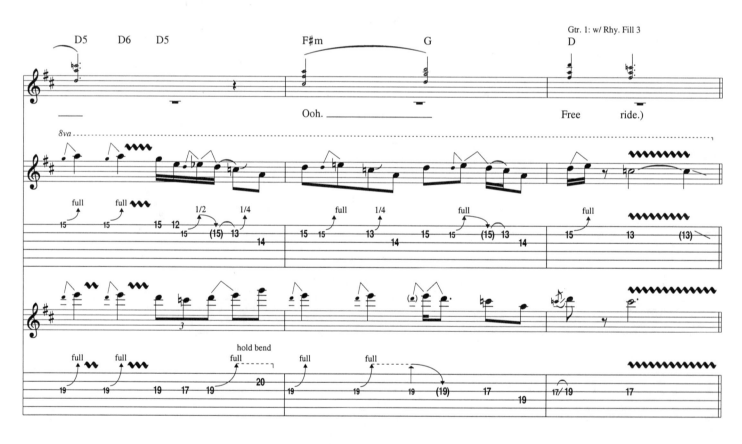

*vib. bent note only

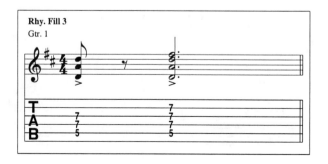

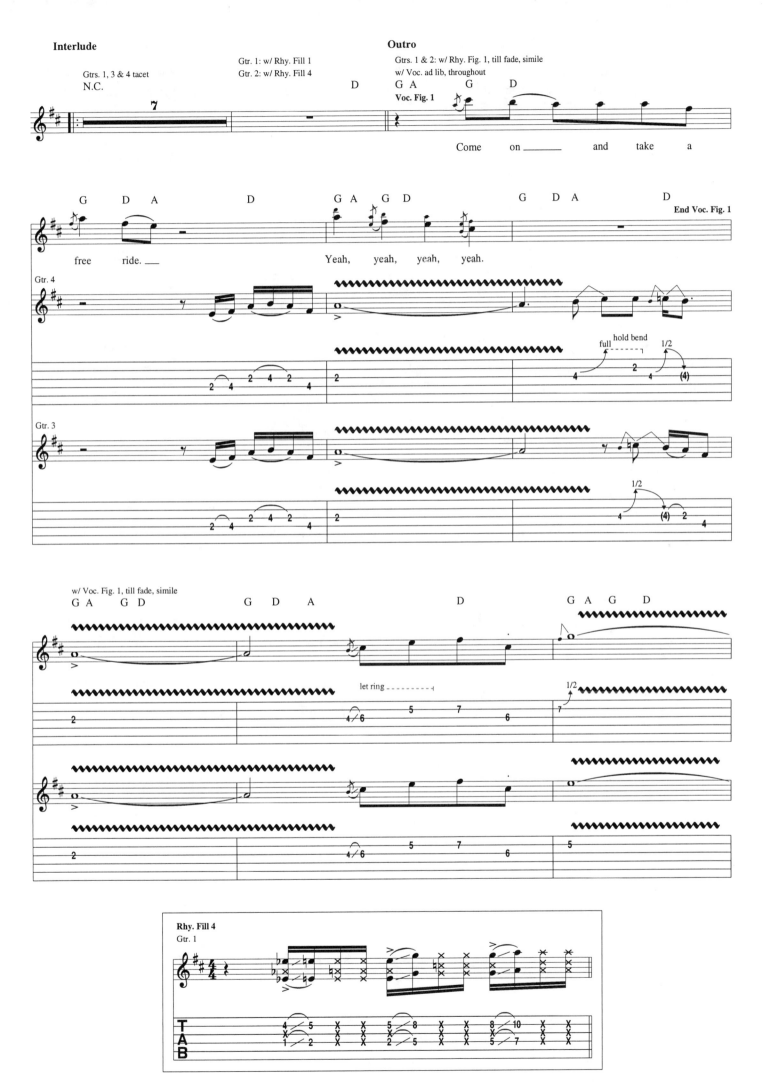

Gtr. 1: w/ Rhy. Fill 5

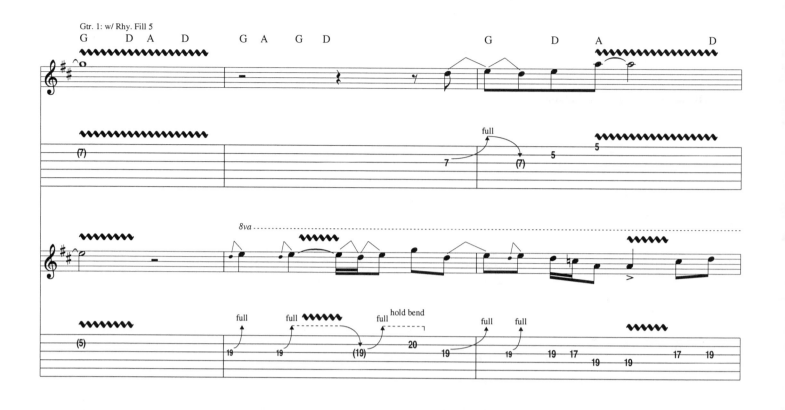

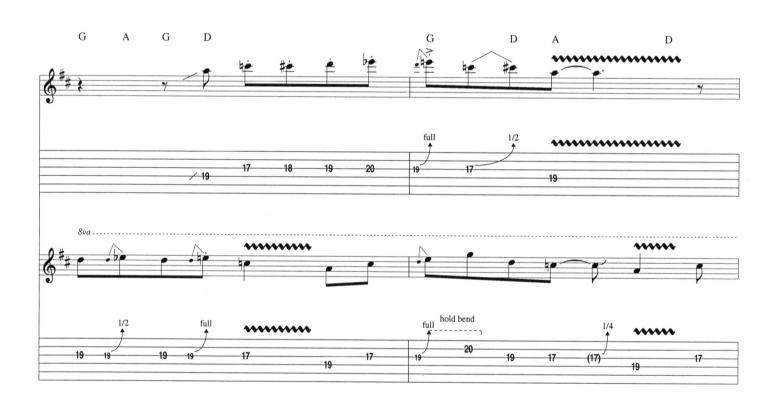

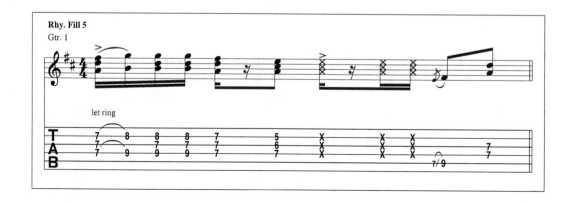

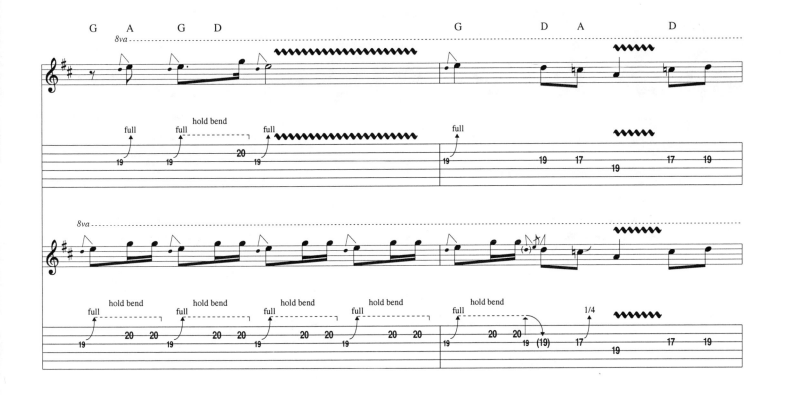

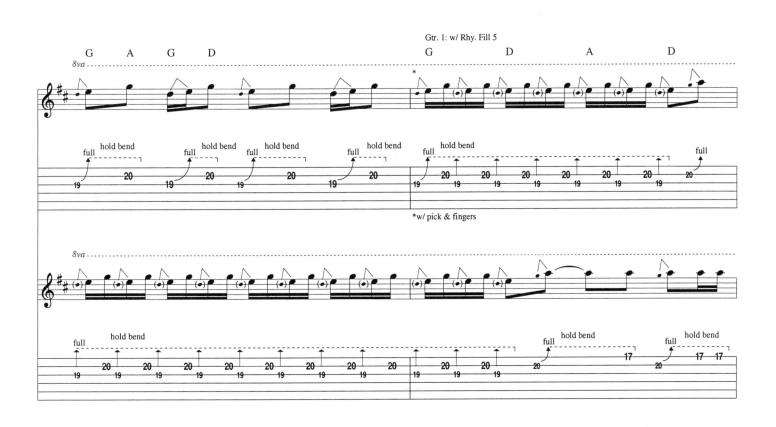

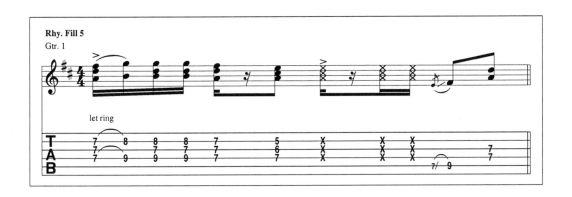

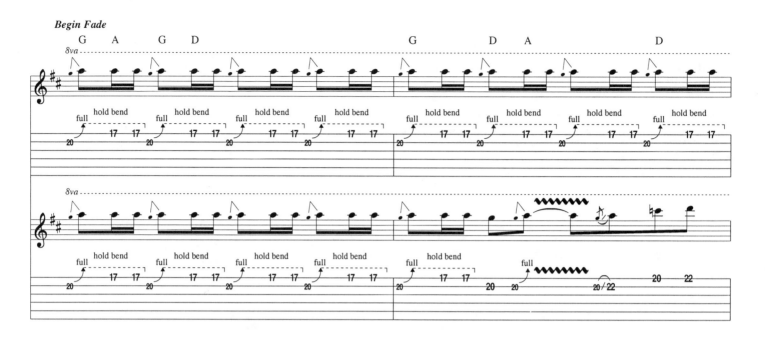

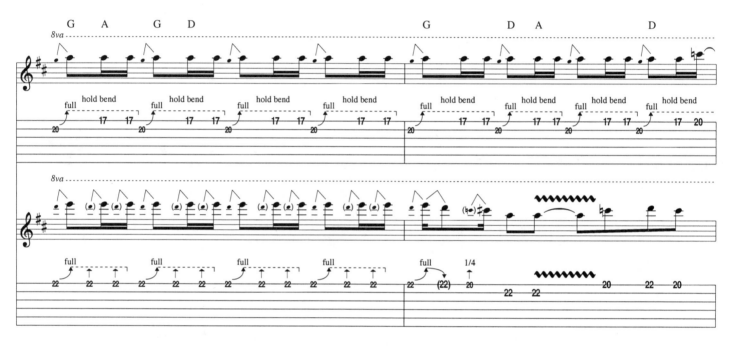

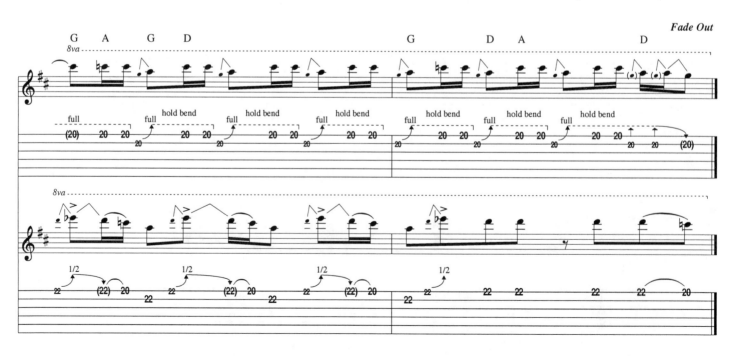

# Godzilla

**Words and Music by Donald Roeser**

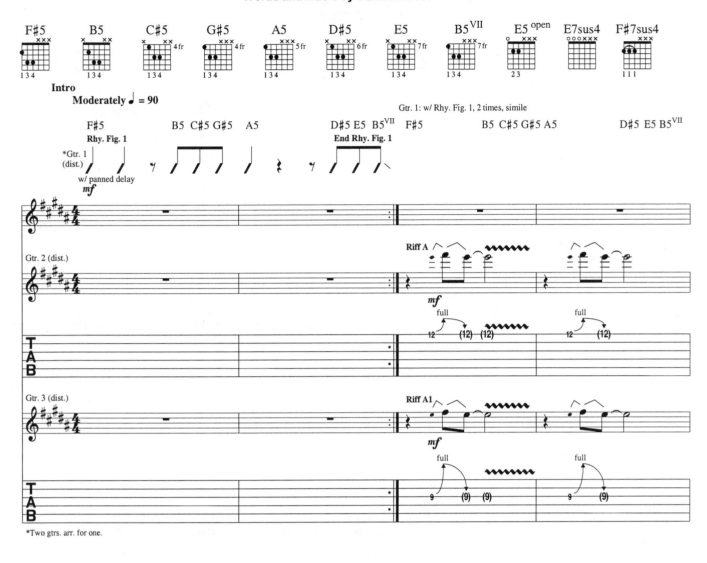

*Two gtrs. arr. for one.

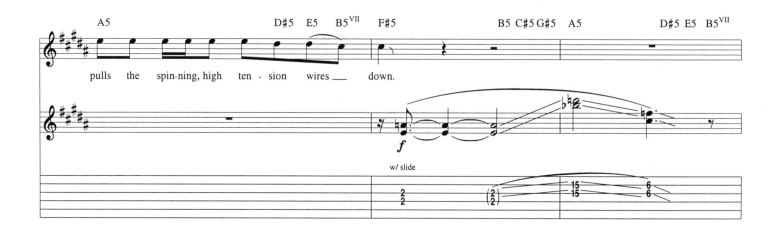

pulls the spin-ning, high ten - sion wires \_\_\_ down.

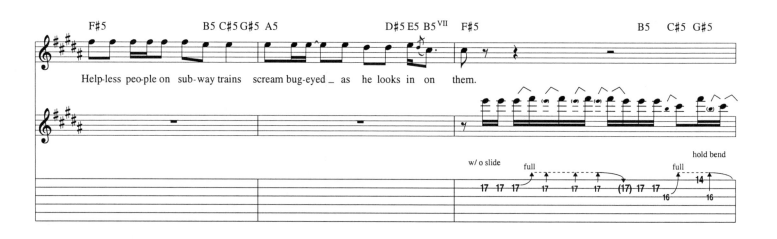

Help-less peo-ple on sub-way trains scream bug-eyed \_ as he looks in on them.

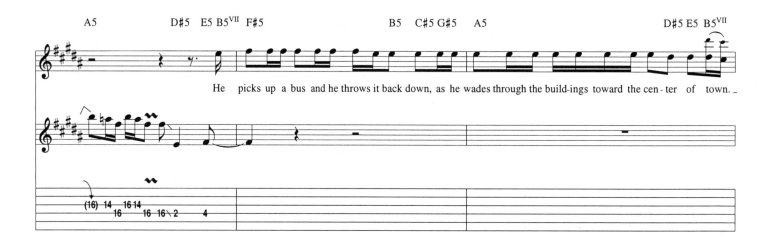

He picks up a bus and he throws it back down, as he wades through the build-ings toward the cen - ter of town. \_

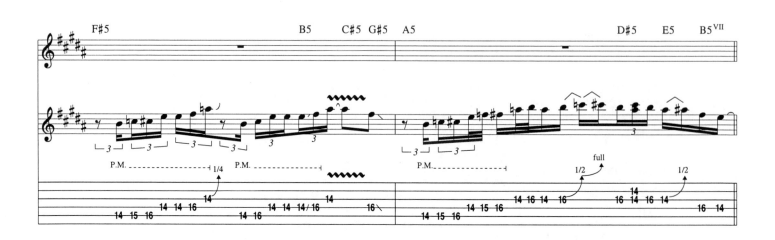

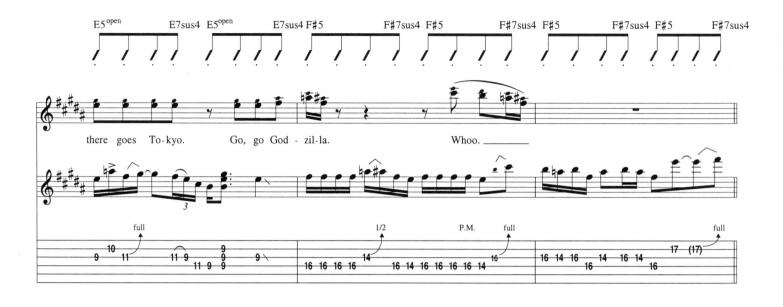

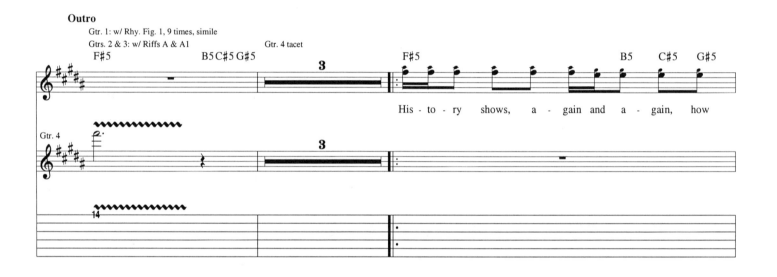

**Outro**

Gtr. 1: w/ Rhy. Fig. 1, 9 times, simile
Gtrs. 2 & 3: w/ Riffs A & A1

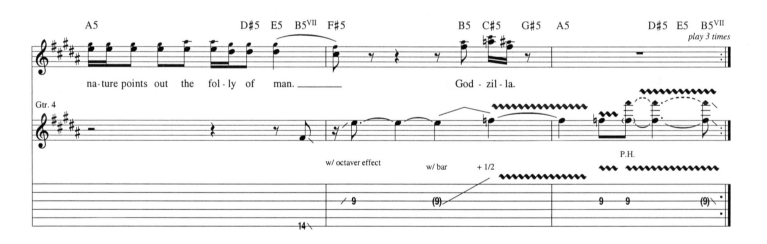

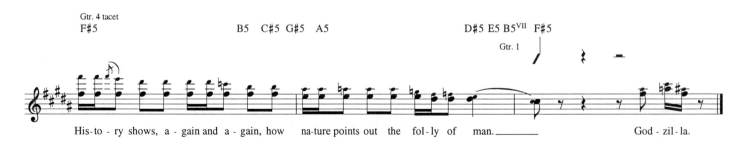

# Hair of the Dog

**Words and Music by Dan McCafferty, Darrell Sweet, Pete Agnew and Manuel Charlton**

**Intro**

Moderate Rock ♩ = 128

1. Heart break - er, soul shak - er, I've been told ___ a - bout you.
2. Talk-in' jiv - ey, poi - son i - vy, you ain't gon - na cling ___ to me. ___

Steam-roll - er, mid-night stroll - er, what they've been say - in' must be true. ___
Man tak - er, born fak - er, I ain't so blind ___ I can't ___ see. }

Red hot ma - ma, vel - vet charm - er, time's come to pay your dues. ___

*composite arrangement
**Key signature denotes E Mixolydian.
***Chord symbols reflect implied harmony.

# Hey Joe

**Words and Music by Billy Roberts**

you know I caught her mess-in' 'round with an-oth-er man.

Yeah!

Ooh.

I'm go-in' down to shoot my old la-dy,

you know I caught her mess-in' 'round with an-oth-er man. _ Huh! And that ain't

too cool.
— )
(Ah. _
2. Uh, hey, _ Joe, _
I heard you, shot your

woman down, you shot her down, now.

Uh, hey, Joe,    I heard you shot your old

Ah.

mess-in' 'round town. ___

C       Gadd9       D       A

Uh, yes I did, I shot her,       you know I caught my old la-dy mess-in' 'round

Ah. ___

Shoot her one more time a - gain, _ ba - by!

Ooh. _____

Hey, Joe! _____ )

Yeah! _____ Ah, dig it!

# Jesus Is Just Alright

**Words and Music by Arthur Reynolds**

# Let It Be

**Words and Music by John Lennon and Paul McCartney**

Whis - per words ___ of wis - dom,    let it   be. ___
Oo,              oo,             oo. _____ Ah.)

*D.S. al Coda*

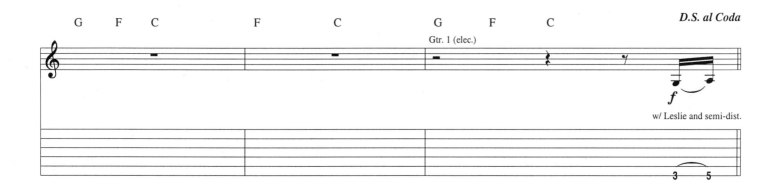

Gtr. 1 (elec.)

w/ Leslie and semi-dist.

## Coda

be, _    hee, _ ah. Let it be, ___   let it be.    Ah, let it be, ____ yeah, let it be. _
oo,          oo.        Oo,        oo,        oo,        oo.)

Gtr. 1

Whis-per words_ of wis-dom,    let it be. _____

rit.

# Mississippi Queen

**Words and Music by Leslie West, Felix Pappalardi, Corky Laing and David Rea**

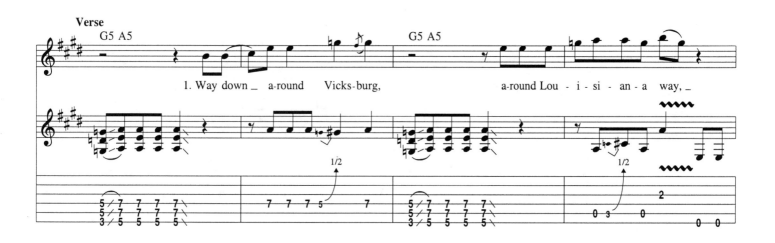

Mis - sis - sip - pi Queen, __ she taught me ev - 'ry-thing.

**Verse**

1. Way down __ a-round Vicks-burg, a-round Lou - i - si - an - a way, __

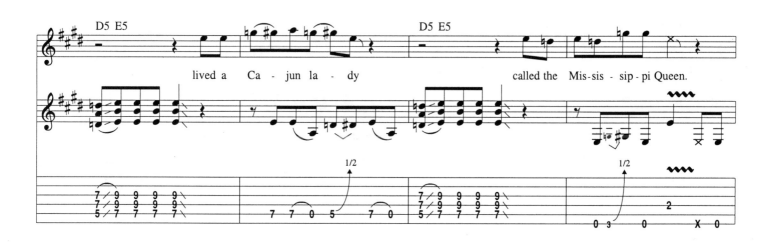

lived a Ca - jun la - dy called the Mis - sis - sip - pi Queen.

You know __ she was a danc - er, she moved __ bet - ter on wine. While the

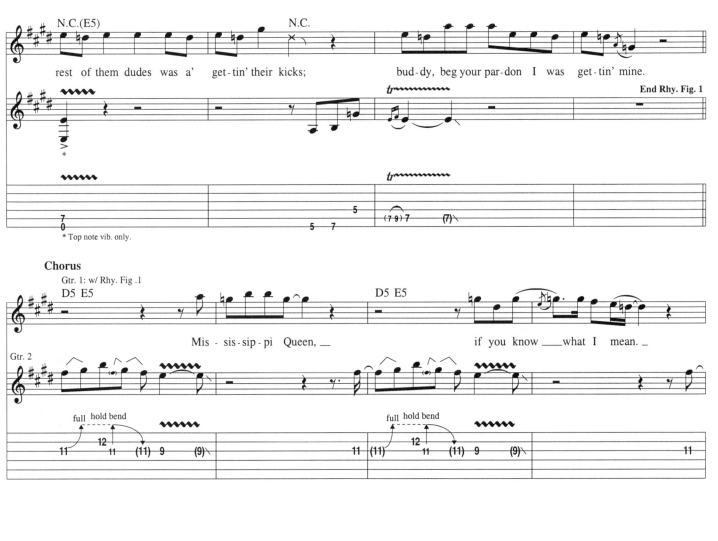

rest of them dudes was a' get-tin' their kicks; bud-dy, beg your par-don I was get-tin' mine.

**End Rhy. Fig. 1**

\* Top note vib. only.

**Chorus**

Gtr. 1: w/ Rhy. Fig .1

Mis-sis-sip-pi Queen, ___ if you know ___ what I mean. ___

Gtr. 2

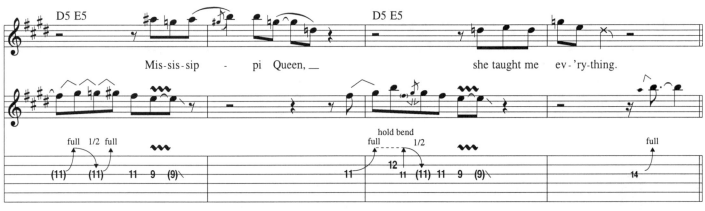

Mis-sis-sip - pi Queen, ___ she taught me ev-'ry-thing.

**Verse**

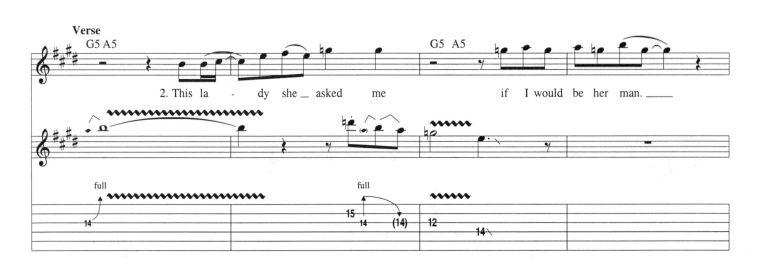

2. This la - dy she ___ asked me if I would be her man. ___

82

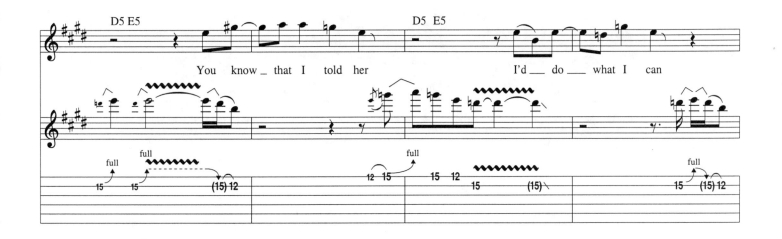

You know __ that I told her      I'd __ do __ what I can

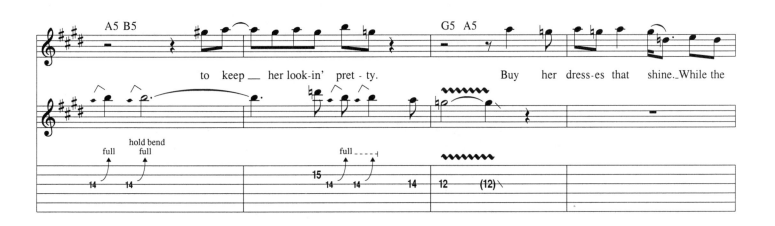

to keep __ her look-in' pret - ty.      Buy  her  dress-es that      shine.__While the

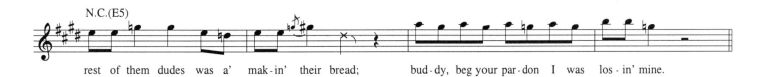

rest  of them dudes  was a'  mak-in' their bread;      bud-dy, beg your par-don  I  was  los - in' mine.

**Guitar Solo**

Gtr. 1: w/ Rhy. Fig. 1, 1st 23 meas. only

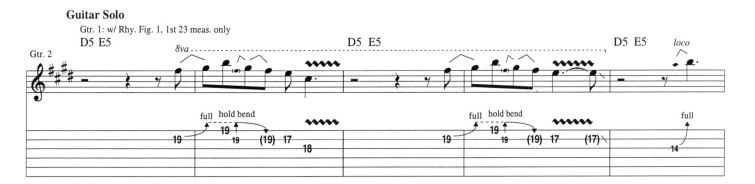

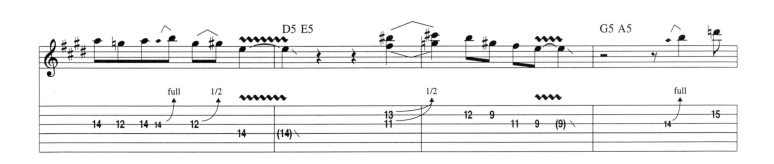

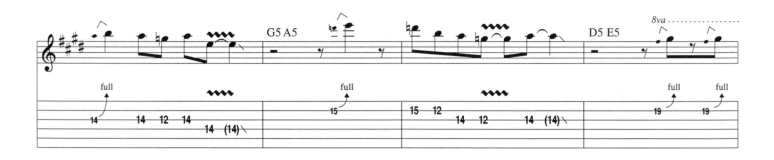

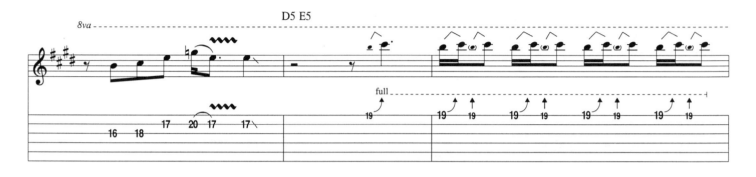

You know __ she was a danc - er, __ she moved __ bet - ter on wine. While the

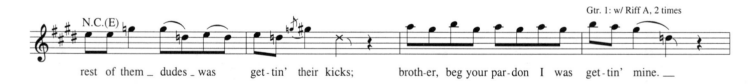

rest of them __ dudes __ was get - tin' their kicks; broth-er, beg your par-don I was get - tin' mine. __

Hey, _____ Mis - sis - sip - pi Queen. __

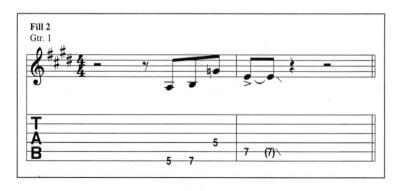

# Money

## Words and Music by Roger Waters

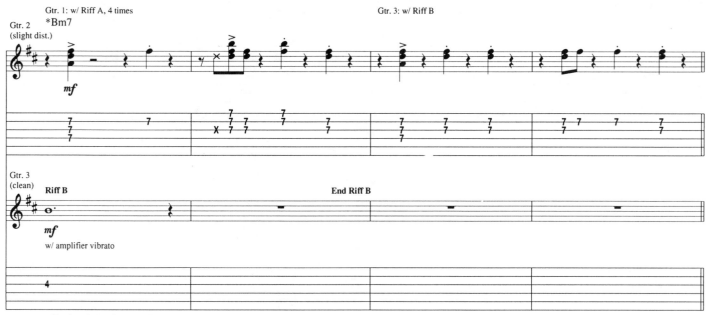

*Chord symbols reflect overall tonality.

good job with more pay and you're o - kay.      Mon - ey, _____      it's a

gas. \_\_\_\_      Grab   that   cash   with   both   hands   and   make    a   stash.

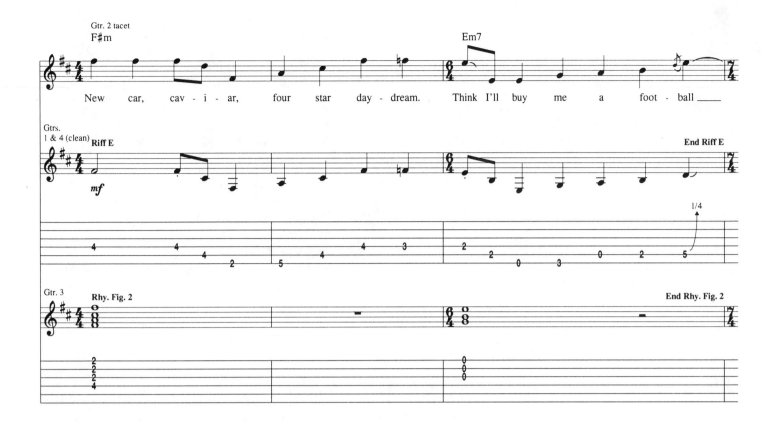

New car, cav-i-ar, four star day-dream. Think I'll buy me a foot-ball ____

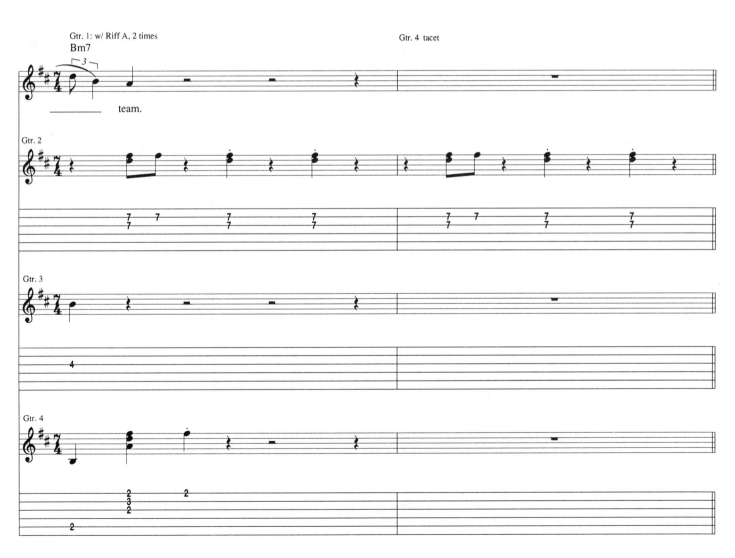

____ team.

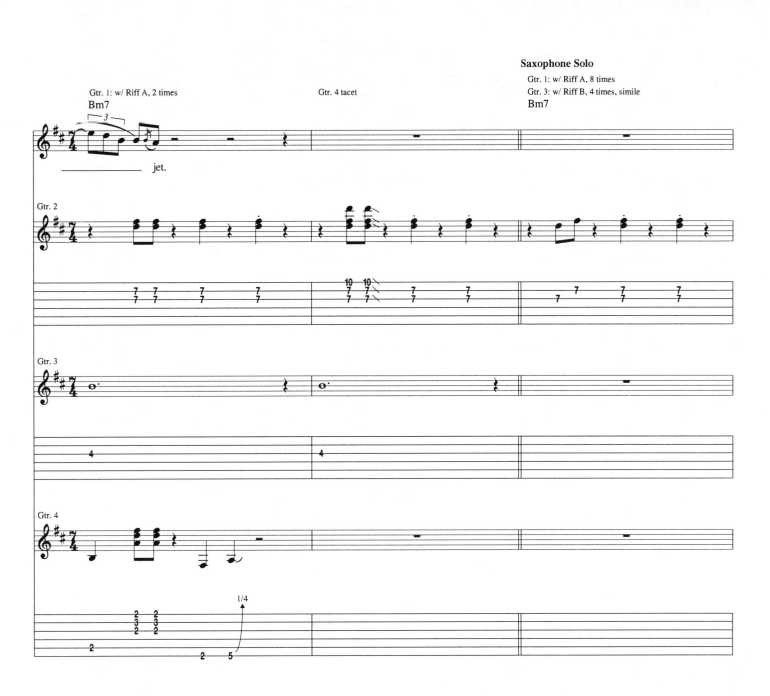

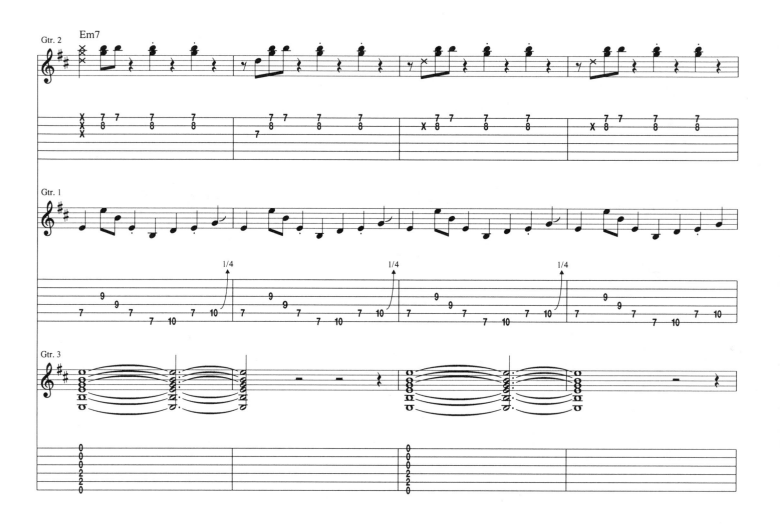

Gtr. 1: w/ Riff A, 4 times
Gtr. 3: w/ Riff B, 2 times, simile

Gtr. 3: w/ Rhy. Fig. 2
Gtr. 2 tacet

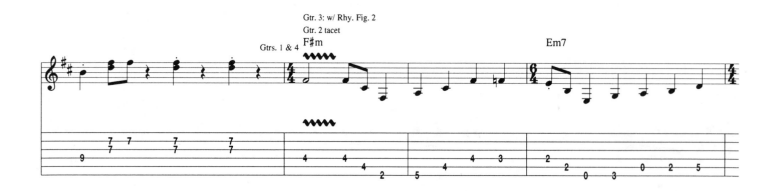

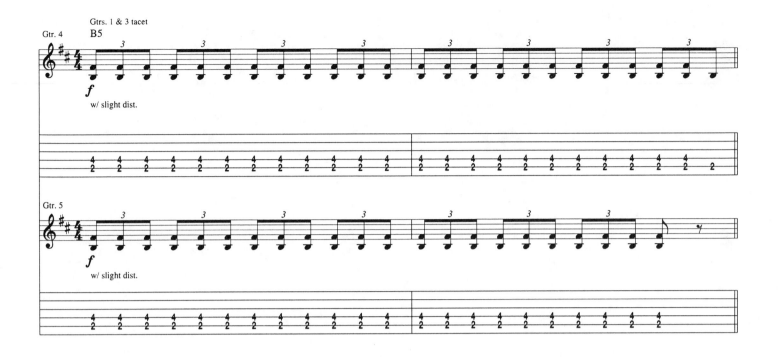

## Guitar Solo

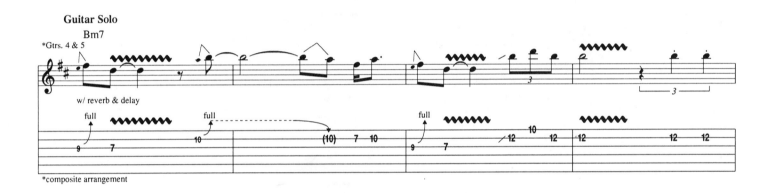

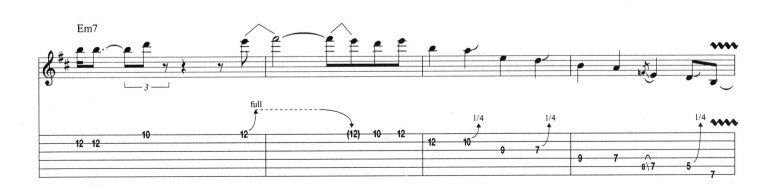

94

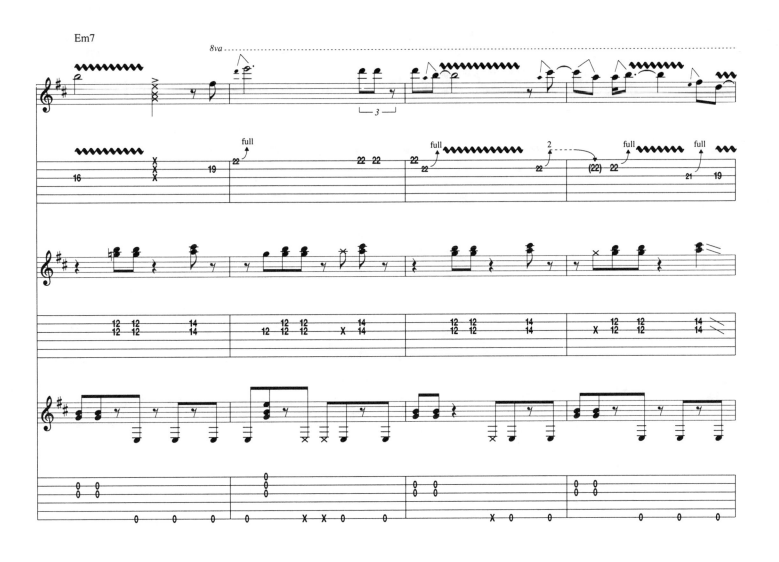

Gtr. 4: w/ Rhy. Fig. 3, simile

**Bm7**

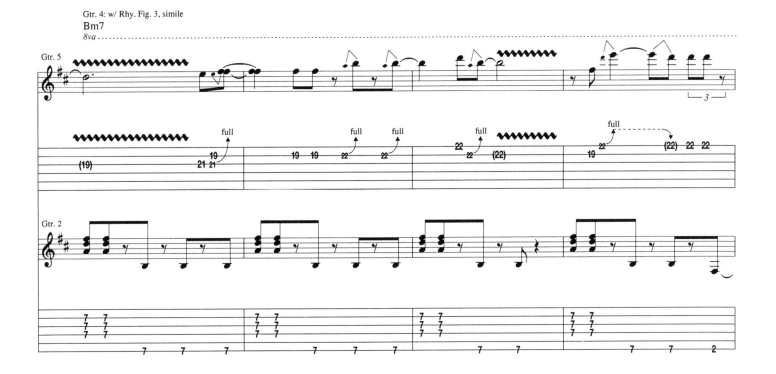

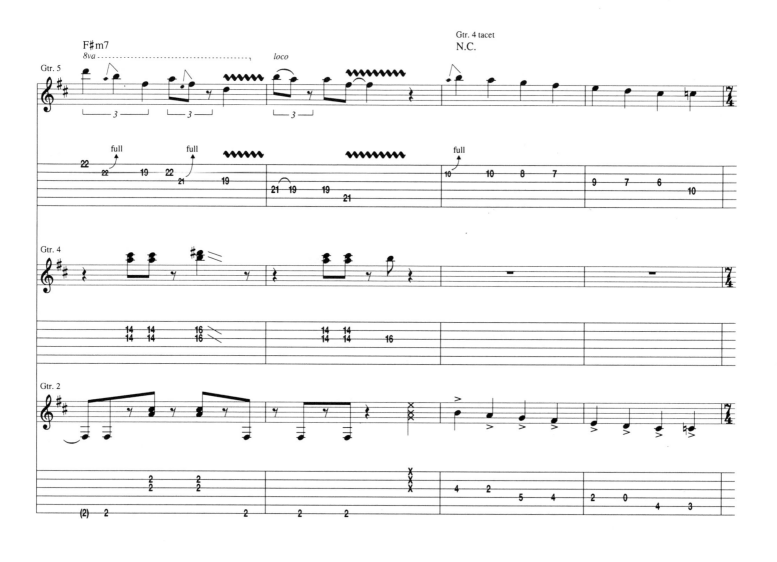

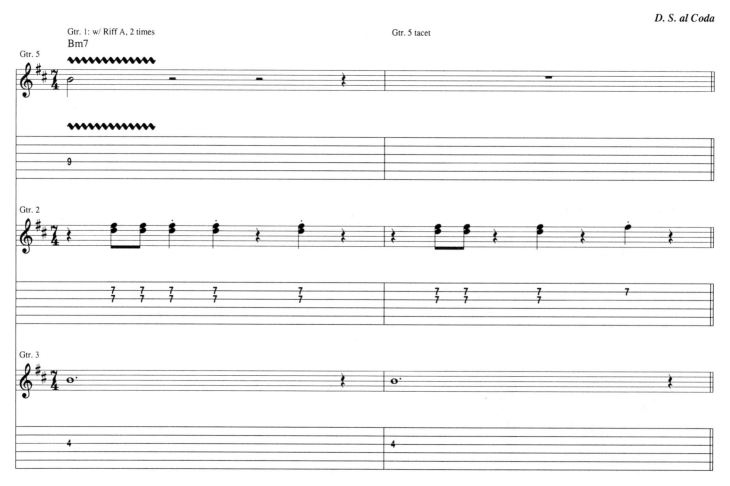

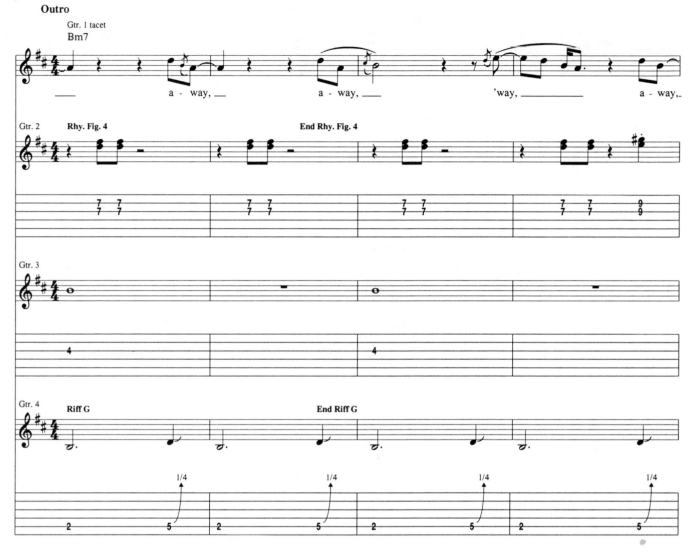

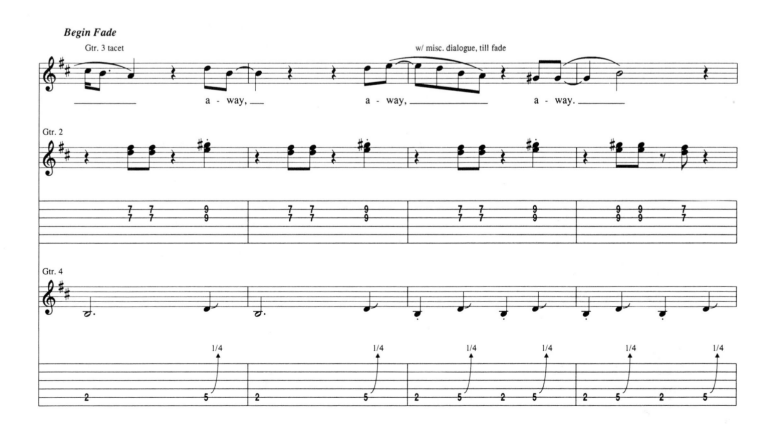

Gtr. 2: w/ Rhy. Fig. 4, 2 times
Gtr. 4: w/ Riff G, 2 times
w/ Voc. ad lib., till fade

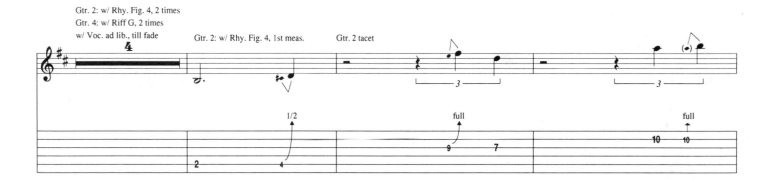

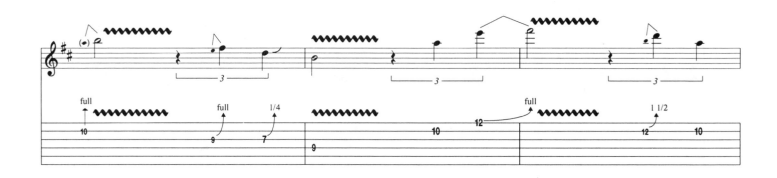

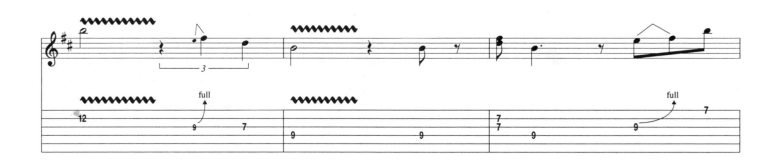

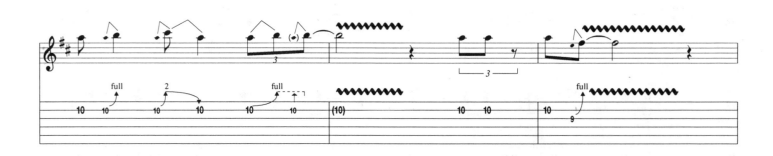

*Fade Out*

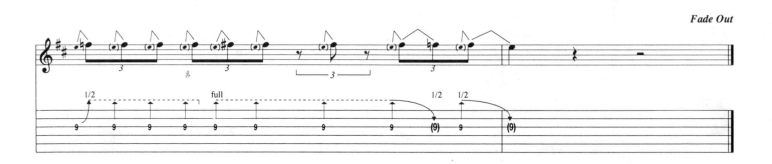

# Piece of My Heart

**Words and Music by Jerry Ragovoy and Bert Berns**

* Vibrato causes F# on 3rd string to sound.

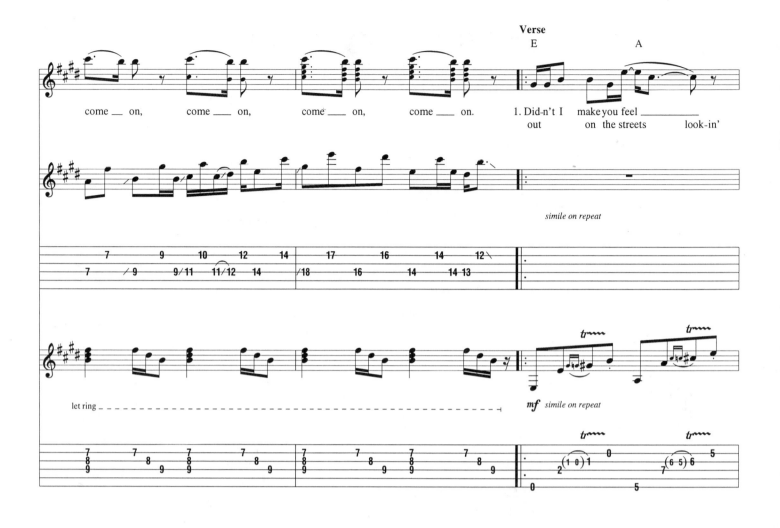

come \_\_\_ on,     come \_\_\_ on,     come \_\_ on,     come \_\_ on.     1. Did-n't I   make you feel _____

out     on the streets     look-in'

*simile on repeat*

*let ring* \_ \_ \_ \_ \_ \_ \_ \_ \_ \_ \_ \_ \_ \_ \_ \_ \_ \_ \_ \_ \_ \_ \_ \_ \_ \_ \_ \_ \_ \_ \_ \_ \_ \_     *mf* *simile on repeat*

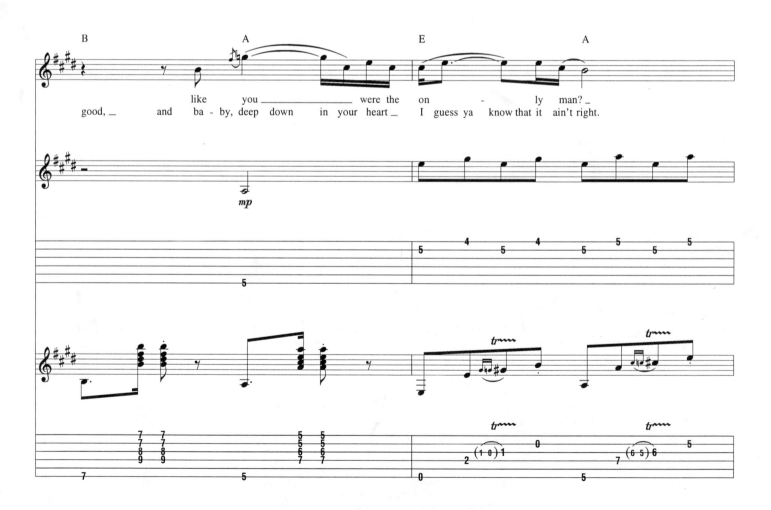

like    you _____ were the    on -     ly   man? \_     I   guess ya   know that it   ain't right.

good, \_     and   ba - by, deep down    in your heart \_

*mp*

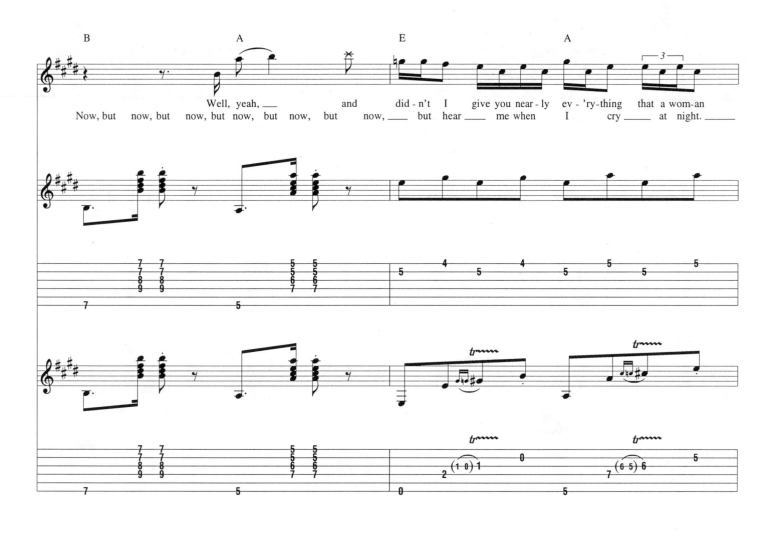

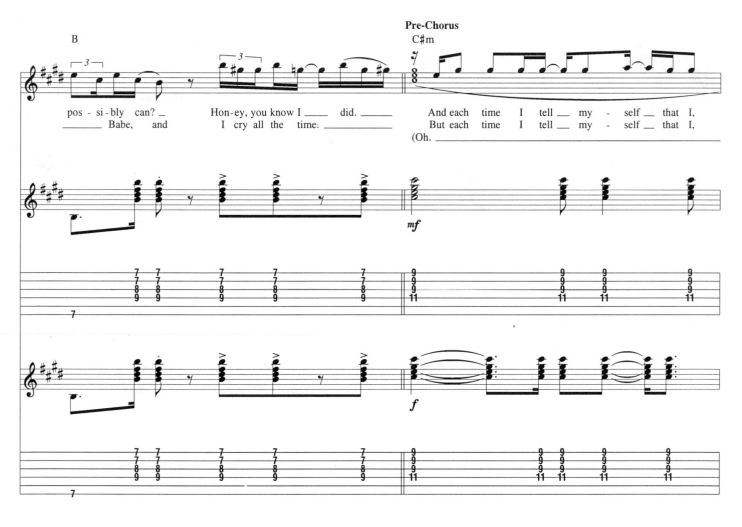

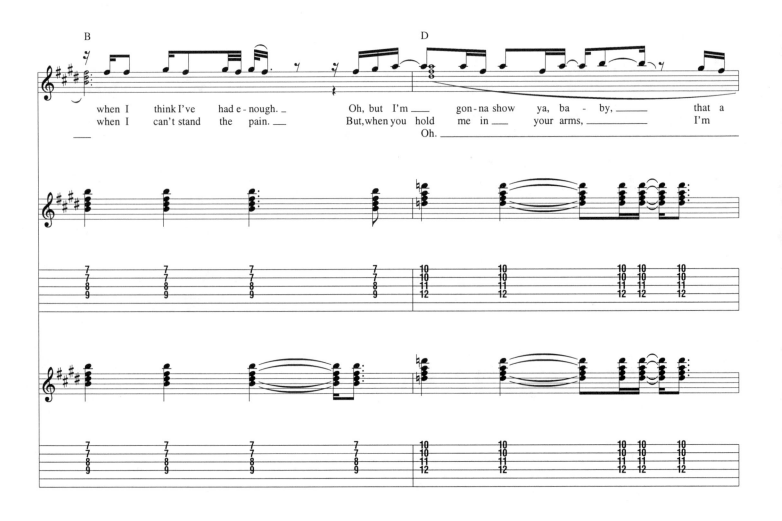

when I    think I've    had e - nough. _               Oh, but I'm ___          gon - na show    ya,   ba - by, ___                    that a
when I    can't stand    the pain. _                    But, when you hold    me in ___        your arms, ___                    I'm
_                                                                Oh. _____

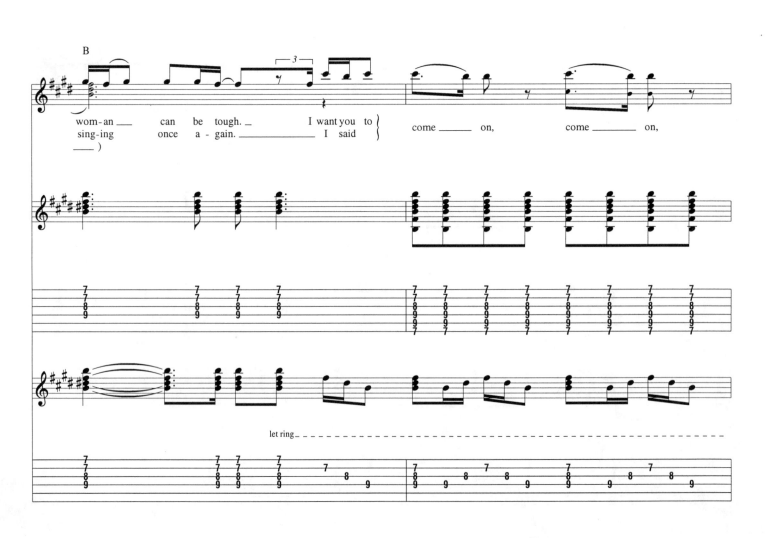

wom-an ___    can    be   tough. _               I want you to }       come ___   on,              come ___    on,
sing-ing    once   a - gain. _____ I said    }
___ )

let ring _ _ _ _ _ _ _ _ _ _ _ _ _ _ _ _ _ _ _ _ _ _ _ _ _ _ _ _ _ _ _ _ _ _ _ _ _ _ _ _ _ _ _ _ _ _ _

Have an-oth-er lit-tle piece of my heart, ___ now, ba - by. ___ Well, you know you got ___ it if it

have a...)

makes you feel good, _ oh, yes in - deed. _

2. You're

**Chorus**

Gtrs. 1 & 2: w/ Rhy. Figs. 1 & 1A, simile
Bkgd. Voc.: w/ Voc. Fig. 1

take it.    Take an - oth - er   lit - tle piece of   my   heart, _____ now,   ba - by. _____

Break an - oth - er   lit - tle bit off   my   heart, __ now,   dar - lin', yeah, __ come on __ now.

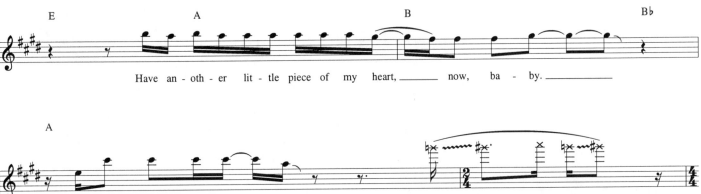

Have an - oth - er   lit - tle piece of   my   heart, _____ now,   ba - by. _____

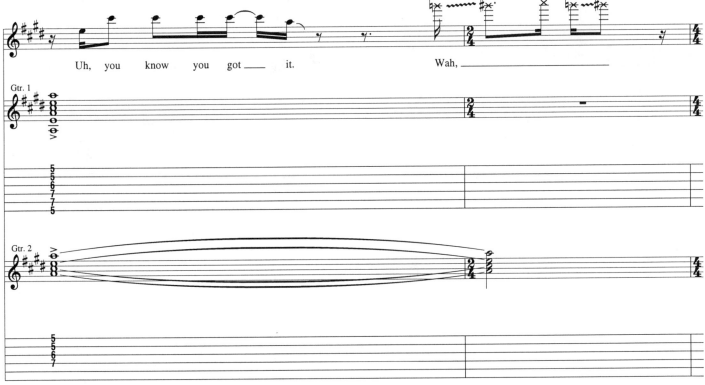

Uh,   you   know   you   got ___ it.                    Wah, _____

Gtrs. 1 & 2: w/ Rhy. Figs. 1 & 1A, simile
Bkgd. Voc.: w/ Voc. Fig. 1

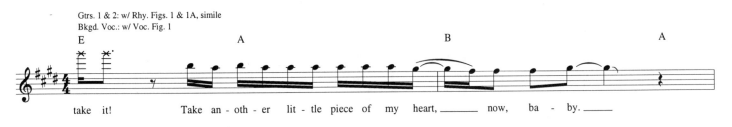

take it!    Take an - oth - er   lit - tle piece of   my   heart, _____ now,   ba - by. _____

# Radar Love

**Words and Music by George Kooymans and Barry Hay**

Bren - da Lee ___ com - in' on strong. ___ The

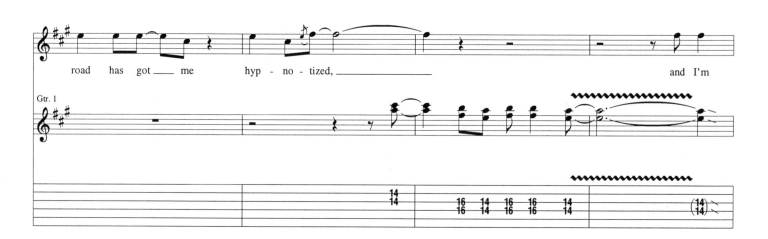

road has got ___ me hyp - no - tized, ___ and I'm

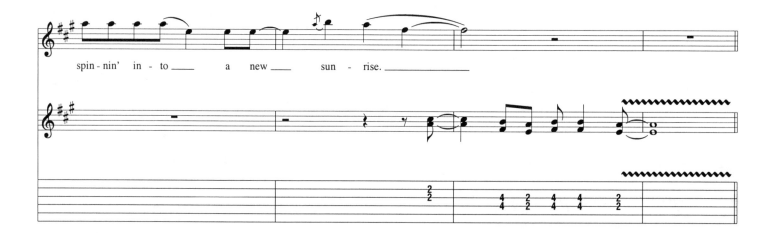

spin - nin' in - to ___ a new ___ sun - rise. ___

## ⅏ Pre-Chorus

Bkgd. Voc.: w/ Voc. Fig. 1
Gtr. 1: w/ Rhy. Fig. 1, simile

E5                                              B5

When I ___ get lone - ly and I'm for sure I've had e - nough, ___

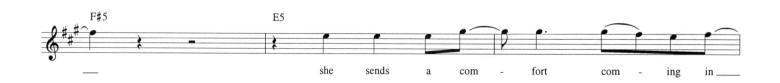

F#5                    E5

___ she sends a com - fort com - ing in ___

B5          A5/B              B5/C#    C#5          B5/C#

___ from a - bove. ___ We don't need no let - ter at all. ___

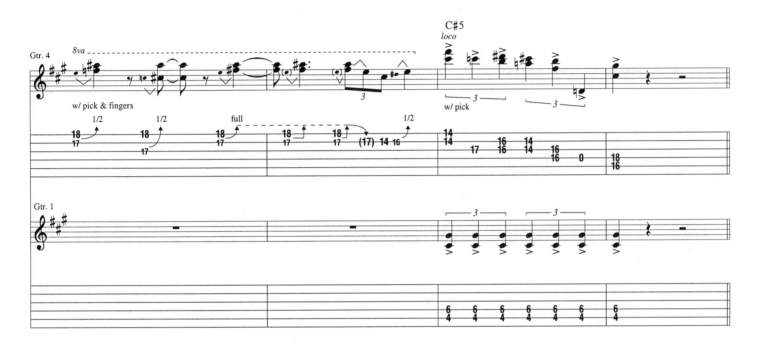

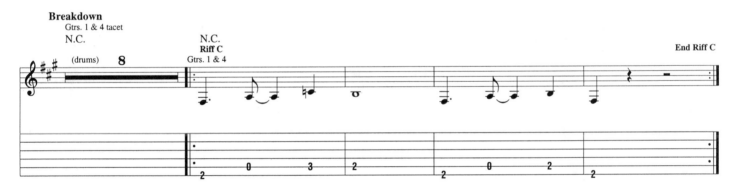

**Interlude**
Gtrs. 1 & 4 tacet
N.C.(F#m7)

Woo!

**Verse**
N.C.(F#m7)

3. No more speed, I'm al-most there.

Gtr. 2

Gtr. 1

Got-ta keep cool, now, got-ta take care.

And the news man sang his __ same song.

*D.S. al Coda*

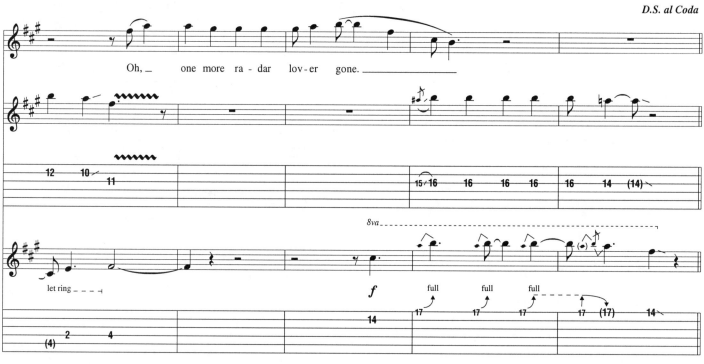

Oh, __ one more ra-dar lov-er gone. __

### ⊕ *Coda*
**Chorus**

Gtr. 1: w/ Rhy. Fig. 2, 1st 4 meas., 2 times, simile

We've __ got a thing __ that's called __ ra-dar love. __

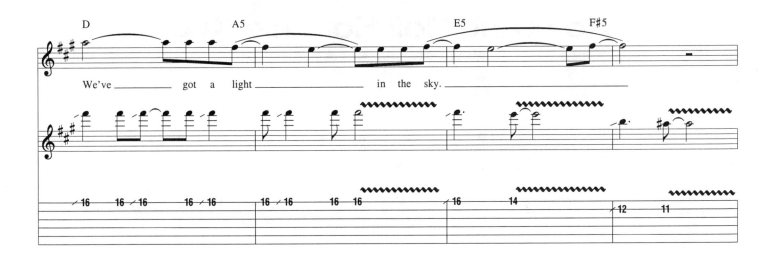

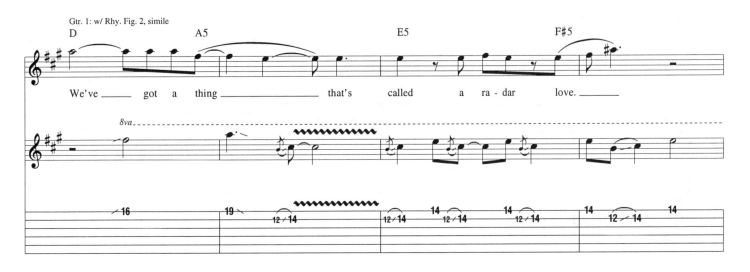

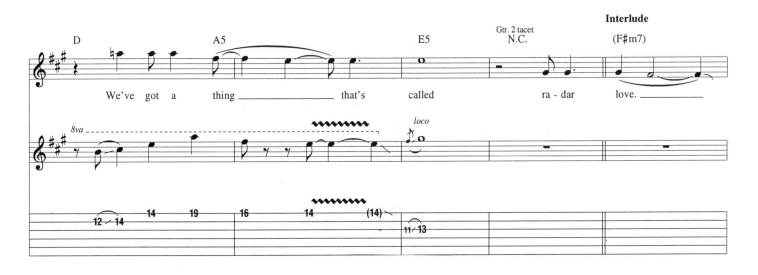

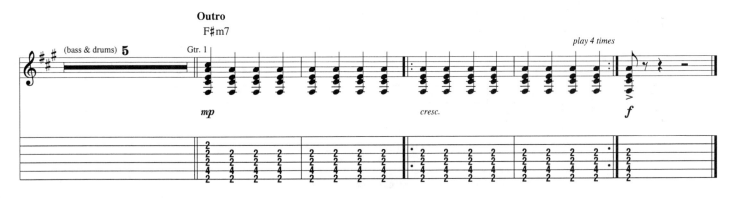

# Rock and Roll Hoochie Koo

**Words and Music by Rick Derringer**

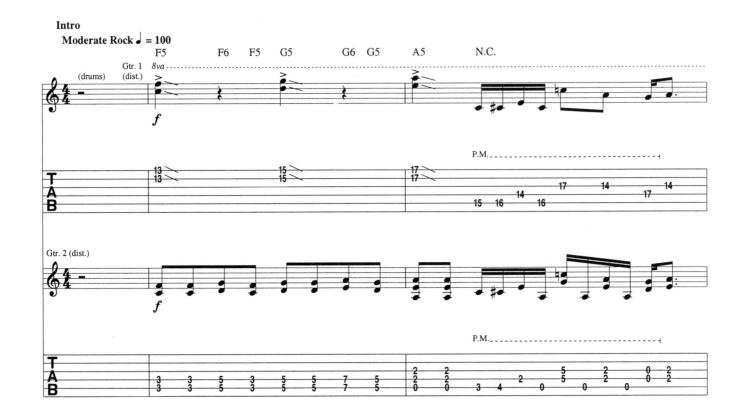

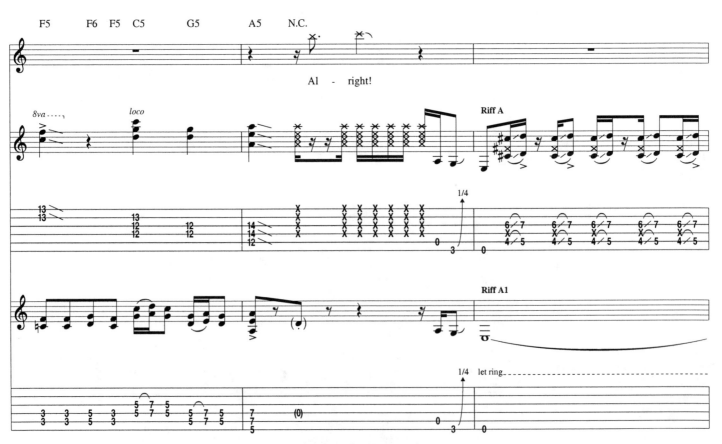

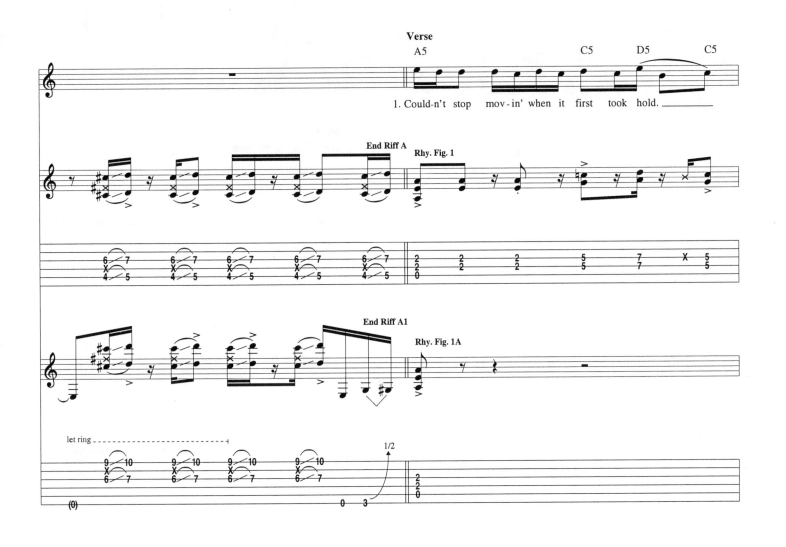

**Verse**

1. Could-n't stop mov-in' when it first took hold.

It was a warm spring night at the old town hall. There was a

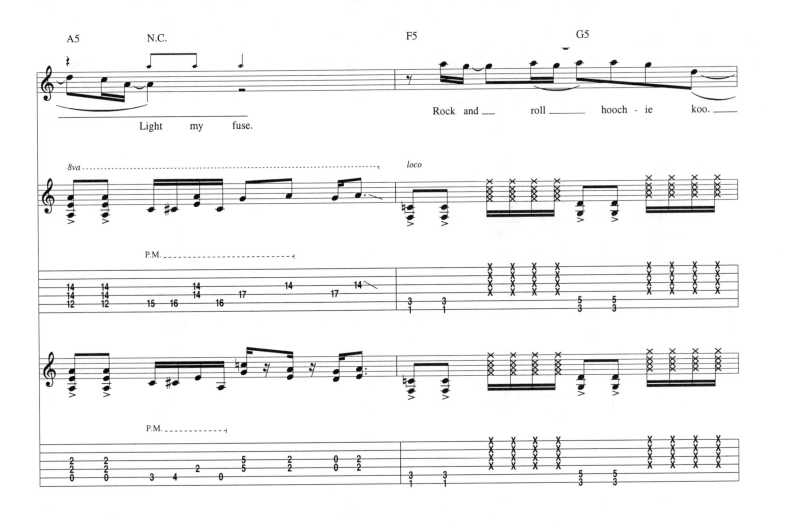

2. Mos -

## 𝄋 Verse

quitoes start-ed buz-zin' 'bout this __ time of year. _____
hope you all know __ what I'm talk-in' a-bout.

I'm
The way you

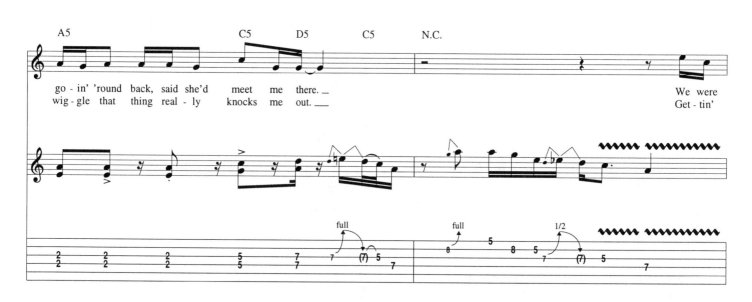

go - in' 'round back, said she'd meet me there. __
wig - gle that thing real - ly knocks me out. __

We were
Get - tin'

rol - lin' in the grass, it was be - hind the barn. _____
high all the time, hope you all are too. _____

Well, my
Come

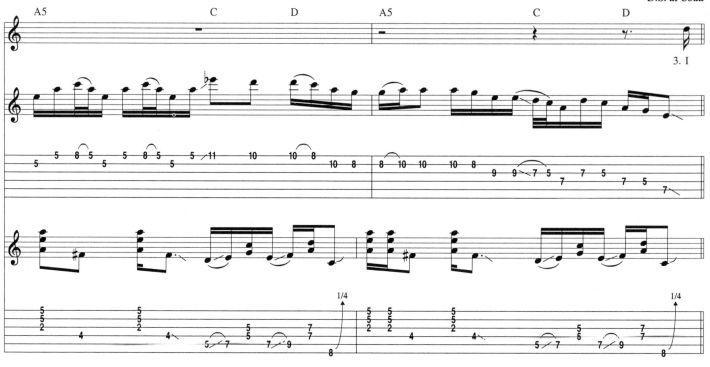

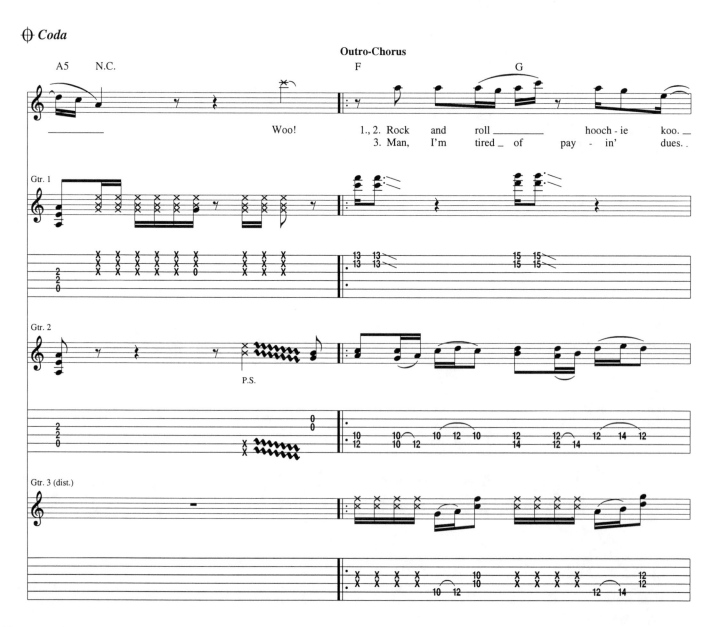

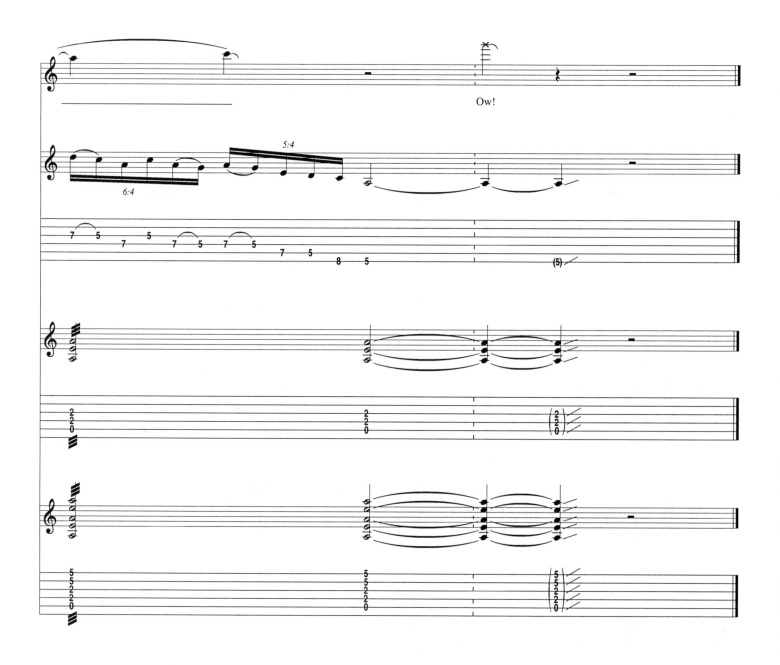

Ow!

# Takin' Care of Business

**Words and Music by Randy Bachman**

# Tumbling Dice

**Words and Music by Mick Jagger and Keith Richards**

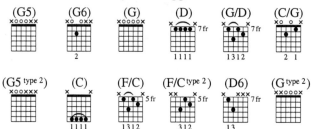

Gtrs. 1, 2, & 3:
Open G Tuning, Capo IV

① = D    ④ = D
② = B    ⑤ = G
③ = G    ⑥ = D

Gtr. 4: Standard Tuning

**Intro**

**Moderately** ♩ = 107

Gtr. 1: w/ Rhy. Fill 1

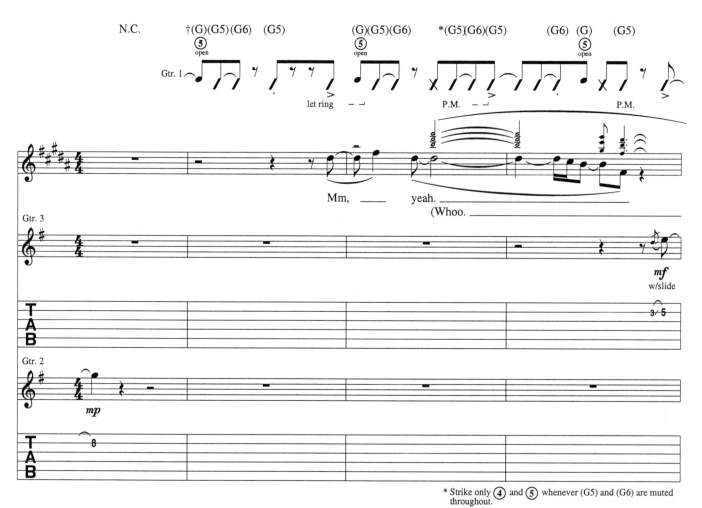

\* Strike only ④ and ⑤ whenever (G5) and (G6) are muted throughout.

† Symbols in parentheses represent chord names respective to capoed guitar when written in slash notation, and do not reflect actual sounding chords.

1. Wo - men think I'm cra - zy but they're al - ways try'n' to waste me, make

me burn the can - dle right down. ____ Ba - by,

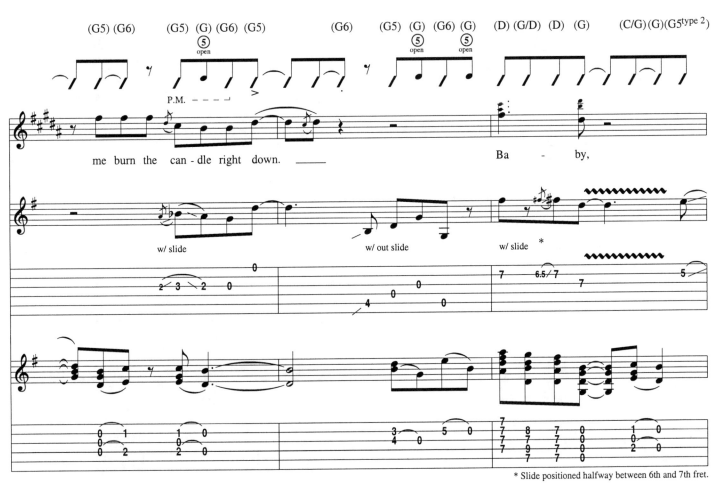

* Slide positioned halfway between 6th and 7th fret.

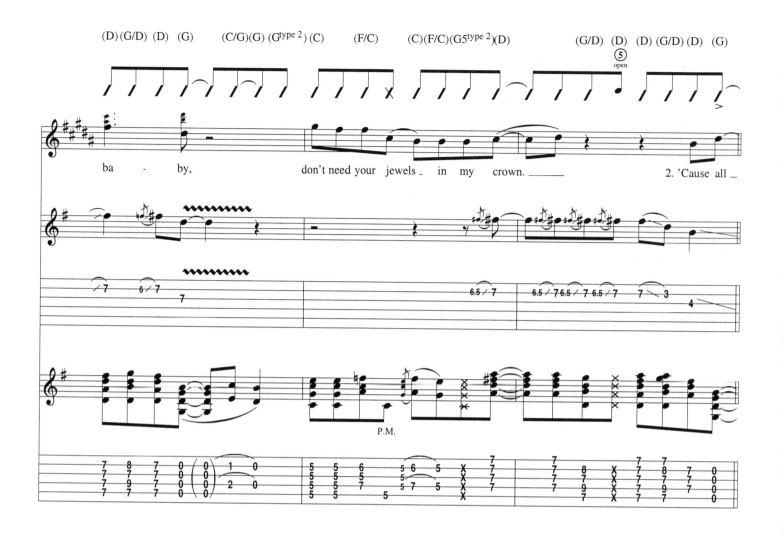

ba - by,　　don't need your jewels　in my crown.＿＿　　2. 'Cause all＿

**Verse**

＿ you wo - men just low - down gam - blers, cheat - in' like I don't know how. ＿

**Rhy. Fig. 1**

**Chorus**
Gtrs. 1 & 2: w/ Rhy. Fill 2

can't stay. You've got to roll _____ me and call me the tum - bl - in'

Harm.

†Symbols in double parentheses represent implied chord names respective to
capoed guitar. Symbols above represent actual implied chords.

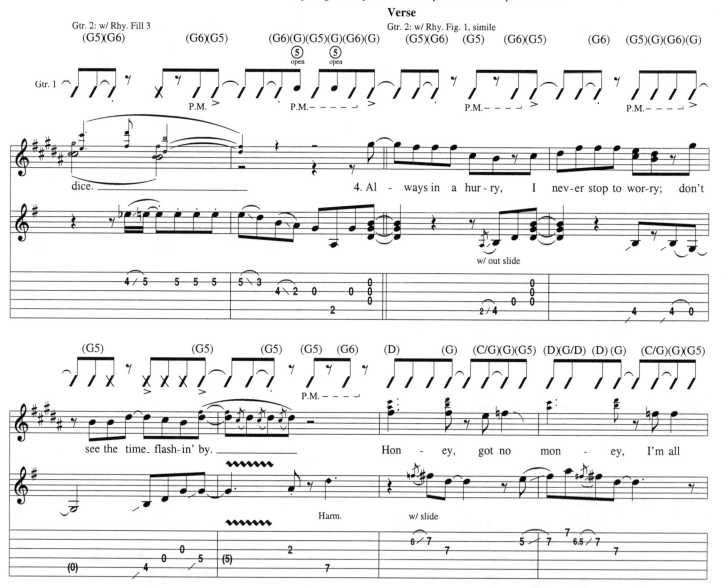

**Verse**

Gtr. 2: w/ Rhy. Fill 3

Gtr. 2: w/ Rhy. Fig. 1, simile

Gtr. 1

dice. _____ 4. Al - ways in a hur - ry, I nev-er stop to wor-ry; don't

w/ out slide

see the time flash-in' by. _____ Hon - ey, got no mon - ey, I'm all

Harm.    w/ slide

**Rhy. Fill 2**
Gtrs. 1 & 2

let ring - - - - - - -

(Gtr. 1: cont. in slash)

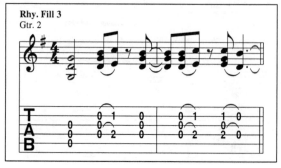

**Rhy. Fill 3**
Gtr. 2

* Gtr. & horns arr. for gtr.

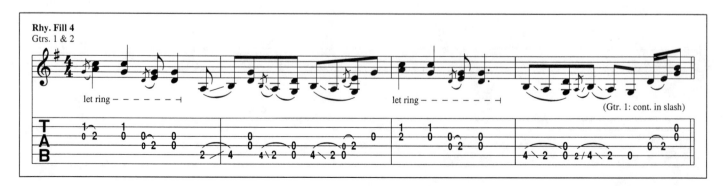

**Out-Chorus**

**Fill 1**

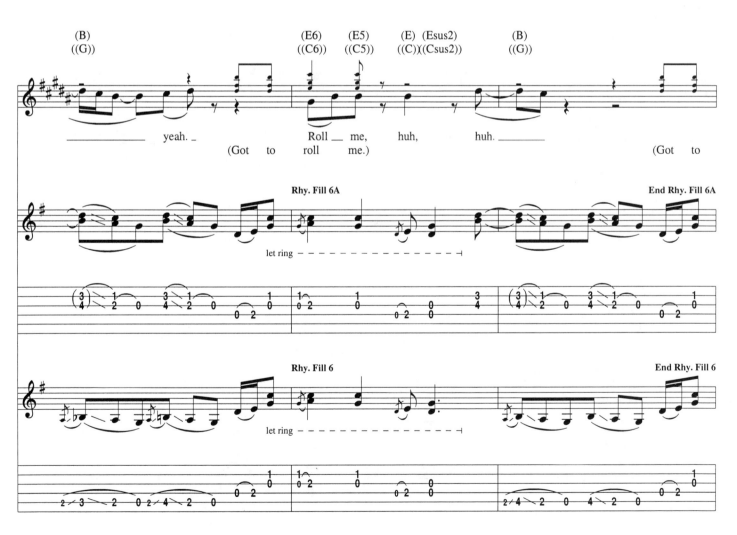

# Two Out of Three Ain't Bad

**Words and Music by Jim Steinman**

I'm tired of words and I'm too hoarse to shout. _  But you've been cold     to   me so   long, _ I'm cry-ing
(Ooh, _____

i - ci - cles in-stead of     tears. _  And all I can do _  is keep on tell - ing you, I
ooh,                ooh.)

## 𝄋 Chorus

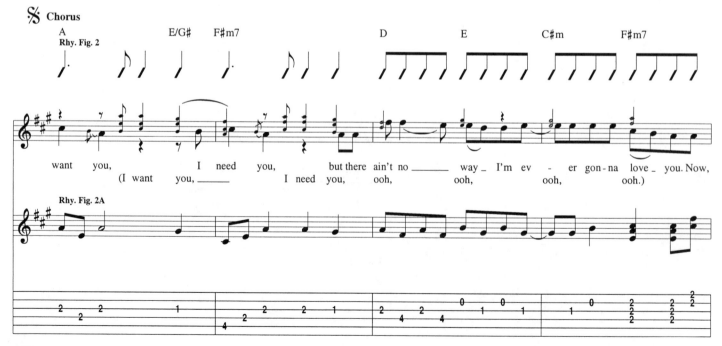

want    you,            I   need   you,      but there ain't no _____ way _ I'm ev - er gon-na love _ you. Now,
(I want    you, _____    I   need   you, ooh,      ooh,        ooh,       ooh.)

ain't no Coupe de Ville hid - ing at the bot - tom of a Crack - er - jack box.
(Ooh, ooh.)

I can't lie, I can't tell you that I'm some-thing I'm not. ___ No mat-ter how I try, I'll
(I can't, uh, lie. _____ Hey.)

nev - er be a - ble to give you some-thing, some-thing that I just have-n't got. ___ 2. Well, there's
(Ah, ___ ah.) (Ooh, woh. ___

**Verse**
Gtr. 2: w/ Rhy. Fig. 1
Gtr. 3: w/ Rhy. Fig. 1A

on - ly one girl ___ that I will ev - er love, and that was so man - y years ___ a - go. ___ And

though I know I'll never get her out of my heart, she nev - er loved me back, ___ ooh, ___ I know. Well, I re -

mem - ber how she left me on a storm - y night. Oh, she kissed me and got out of our bed. ___ And though I

# White Room

### Words and Music by Jack Bruce and Pete Brown

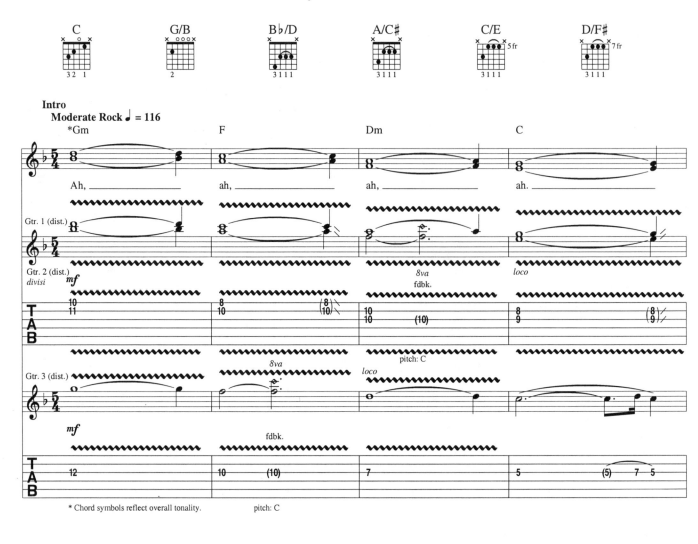

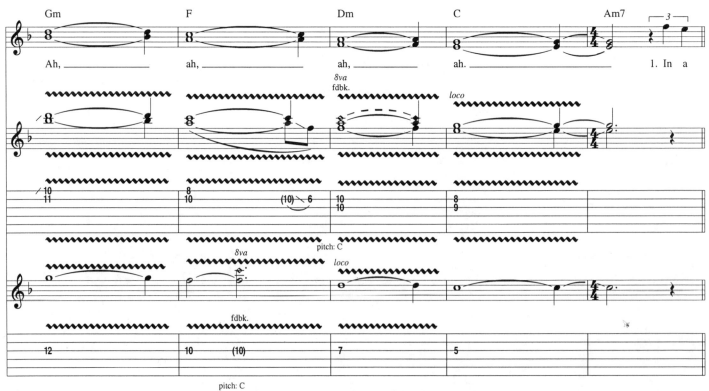

**Verse**

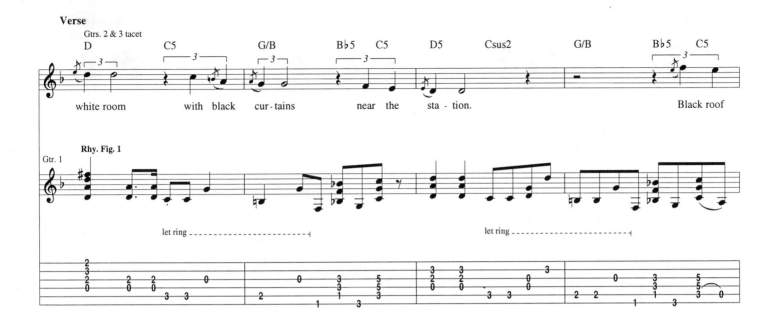

white room     with black cur-tains     near the     sta-tion.     Black roof

coun-try,     no gold pave-ments,     tired ___ star-lings.     Sil-ver

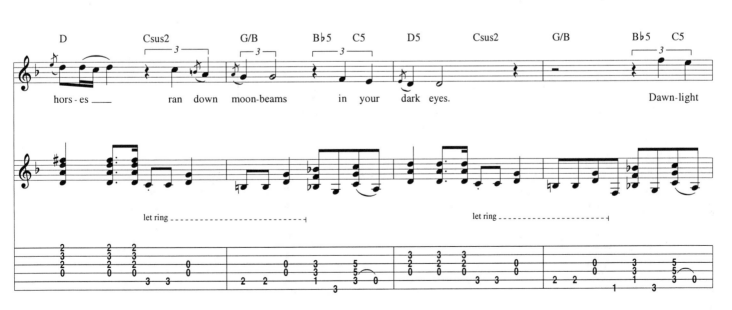

hors-es ___     ran down moon-beams     in your     dark eyes.     Dawn-light

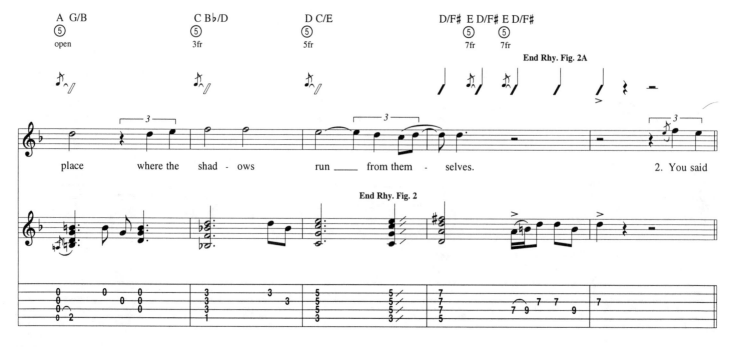

**Verse**

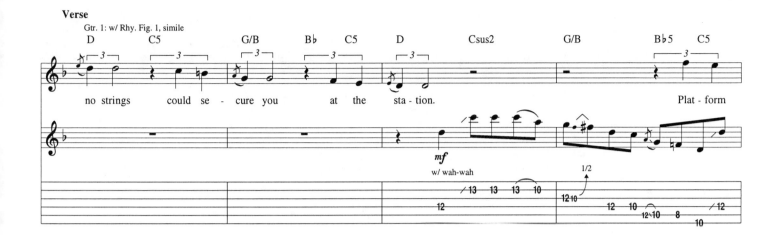

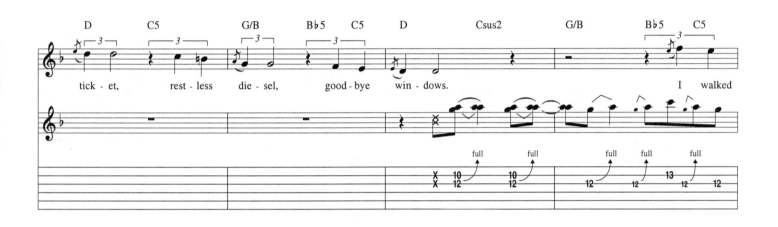

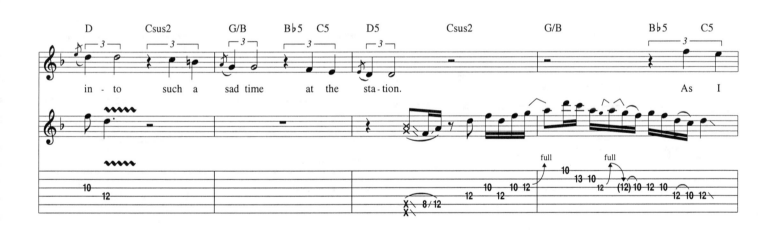

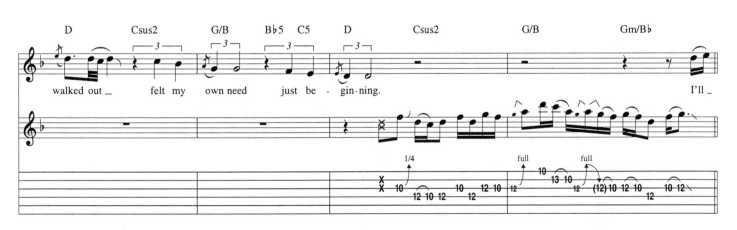

**Bridge**

Gtrs. 1 & 2: w/ Rhy. Figs. 2 & 2A

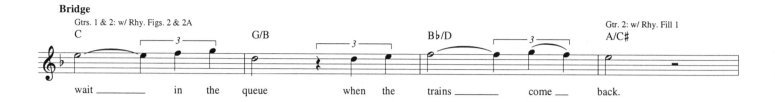

wait ___ in the queue when the trains ___ come ___ back.

Lie ___ with ___ you where the shad - ows run ___ from them - selves. ___

**Interlude**

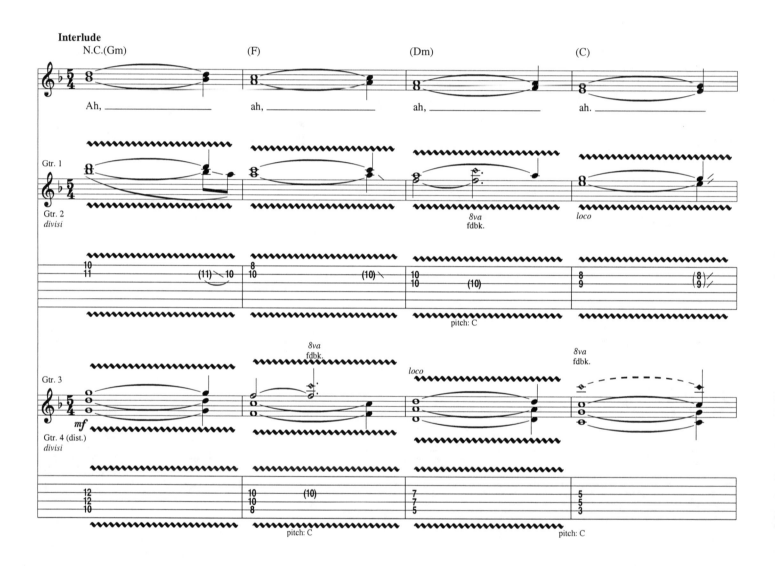

**Rhy. Fill 1**
Gtr. 2

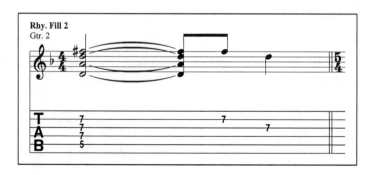

**Rhy. Fill 2**
Gtr. 2

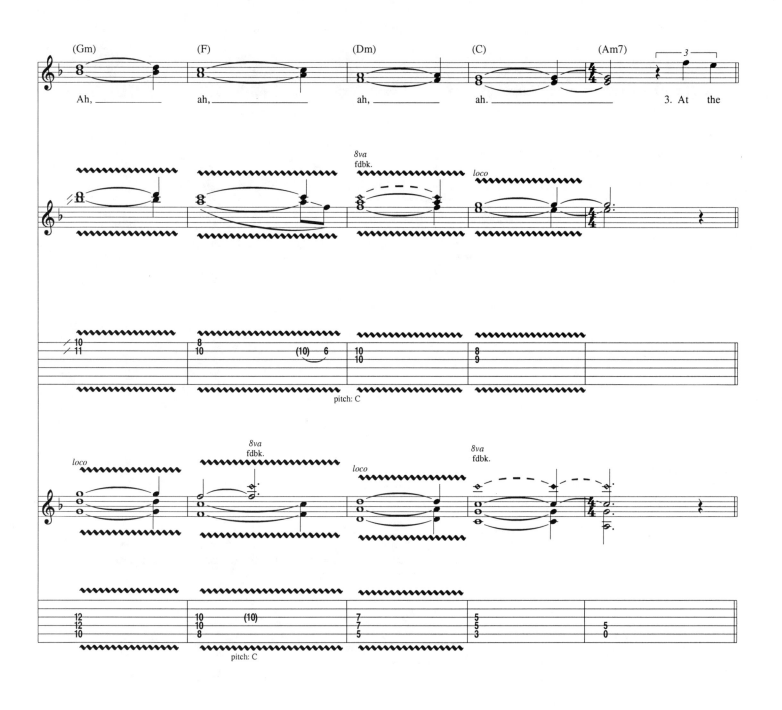

Ah, _____ ah, _____ ah, _____ ah. _____ 3. At the

**Verse**

Gtrs. 3 & 4 tacet
Gtr. 1: w/ Rhy. Fig. 1, simile

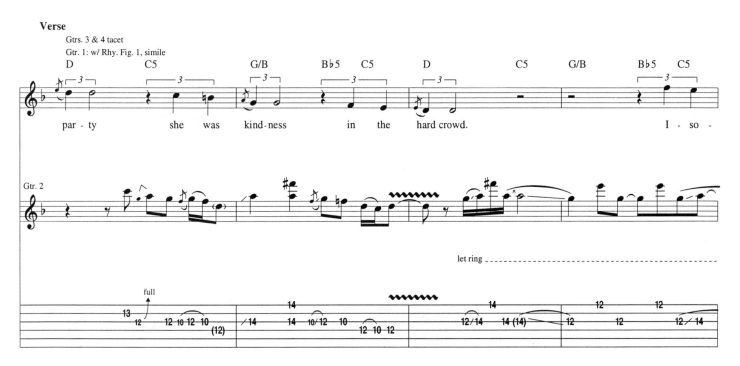

par- ty she was kind-ness in the hard crowd. I - so-

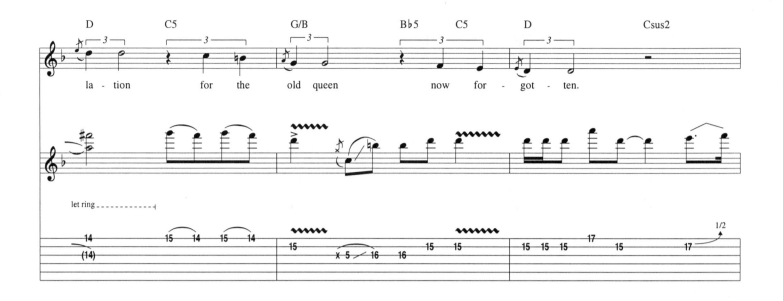

la - tion       for    the     old   queen       now     for - got - ten.

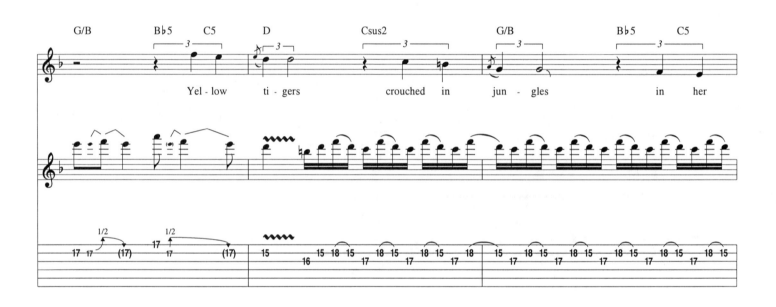

Yel - low   ti - gers      crouched   in    jun - gles       in   her

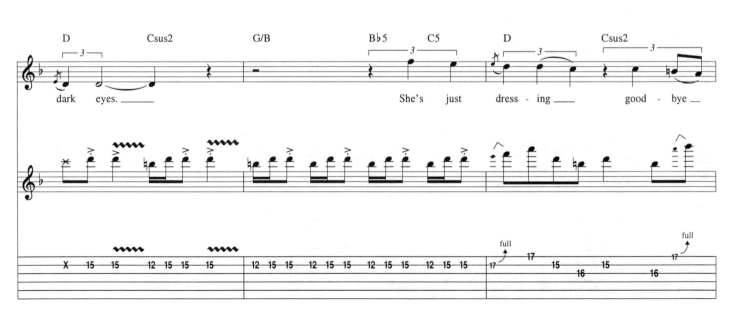

dark   eyes. _____            She's   just    dress - ing ____    good - bye __

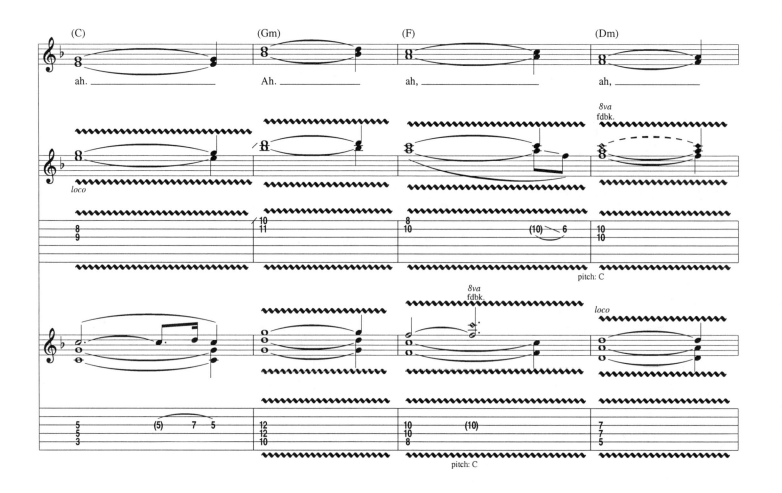

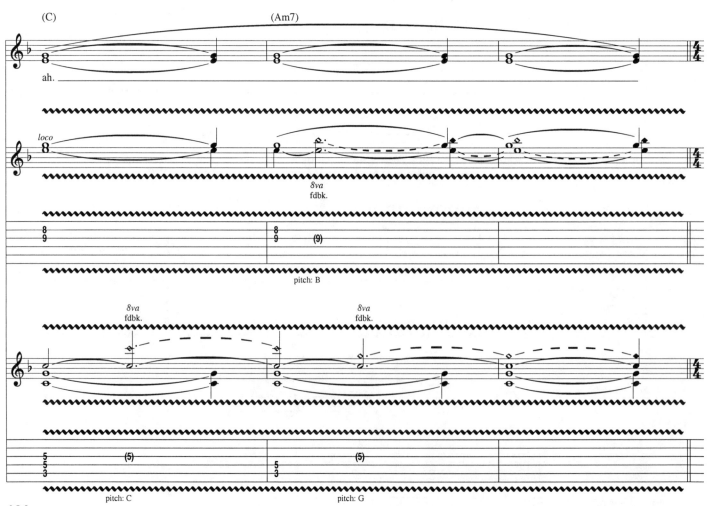

**Outro-Guitar Solo**

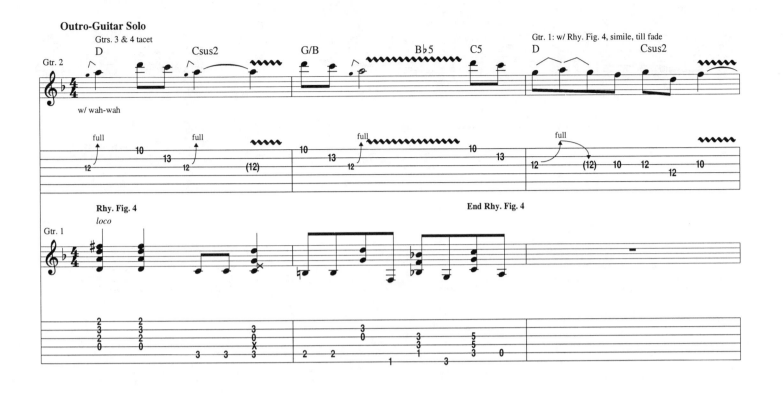

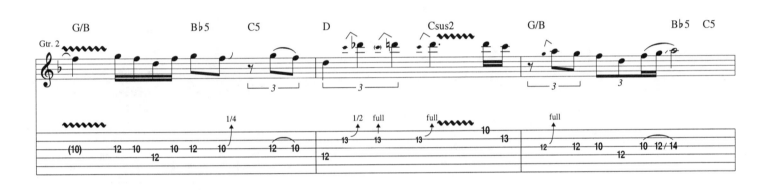

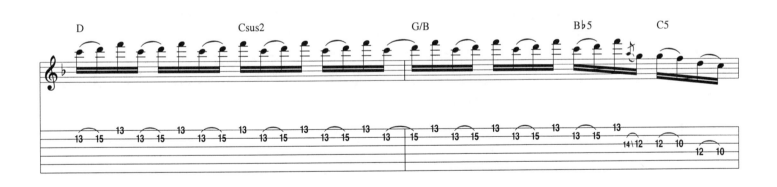

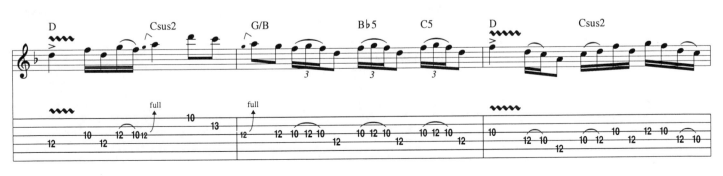

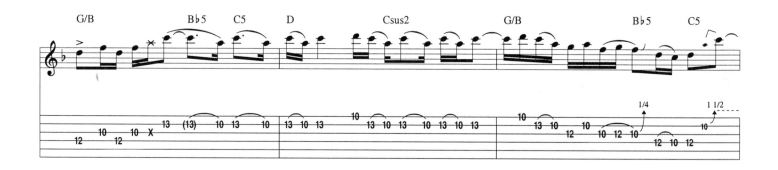

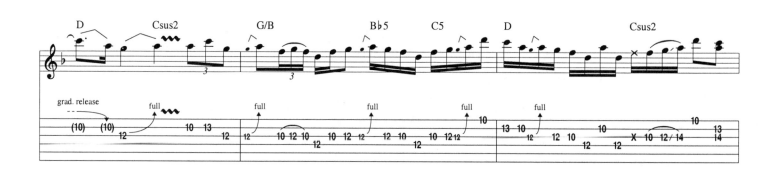

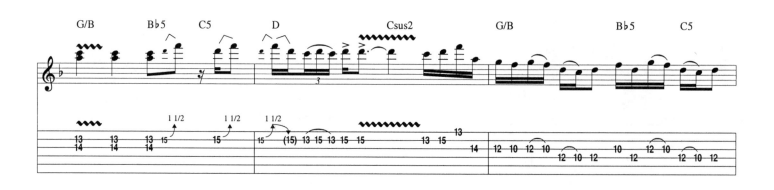

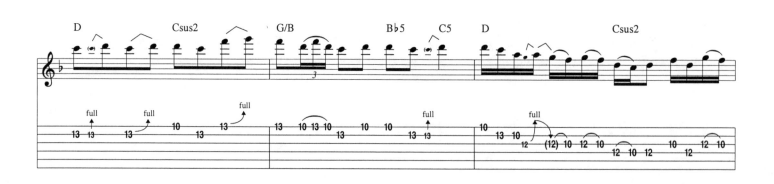

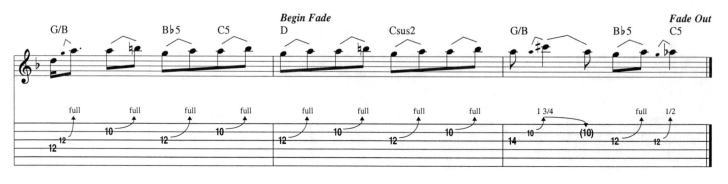

# Woman From Tokyo

**Words and Music by Ritchie Blackmore, Ian Gillan, Roger Glover, Jon Lord and Ian Paice**

**Verse**

**% Chorus**

Gtr. 1: w/ Rhy. Fig. 1, 1st time
Gtr. 1: w/ Rhy. Fig. 1, 1st 7 meas., 2nd & 3rd times    Gtr. 2: w/ Fill 3, 3rd time

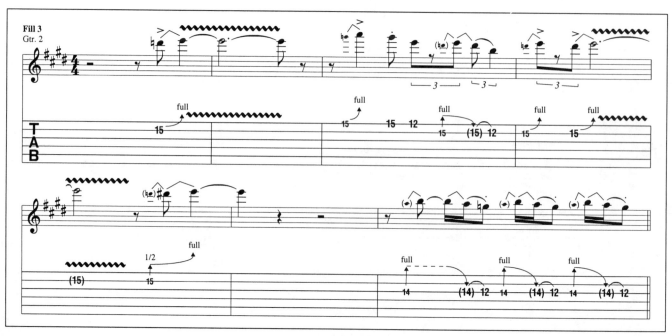

168

Coda 1

When I'm at home an' I, I just don't be - long.

Bridge

So far a - way from the

gar - den we love. She is what

moves in the soul of a dove.

172

# Guitar Notation Legend

Guitar Music can be notated three different ways: on a *musical staff*, in *tablature*, and in *rhythm slashes*.

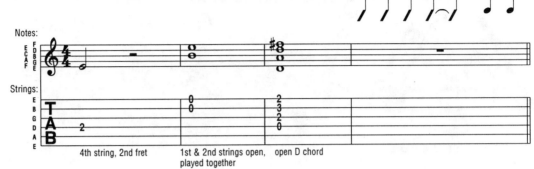

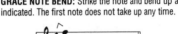

**RHYTHM SLASHES** are written above the staff. Strum chords in the rhythm indicated. Use the chord diagrams found at the top of the first page of the transcription for the appropriate chord voicings. Round noteheads indicate single notes.

**THE MUSICAL STAFF** shows pitches and rhythms and is divided by bar lines into measures. Pitches are named after the first seven letters of the alphabet.

**TABLATURE** graphically represents the guitar fingerboard. Each horizontal line represents a string, and each number represents a fret.

4th string, 2nd fret     1st & 2nd strings open, played together     open D chord

**HALF-STEP BEND:** Strike the note and bend up 1/2 step.

**WHOLE-STEP BEND:** Strike the note and bend up one step.

**GRACE NOTE BEND:** Strike the note and bend up as indicated. The first note does not take up any time.

**SLIGHT (MICROTONE) BEND:** Strike the note and bend up 1/4 step.

**BEND AND RELEASE:** Strike the note and bend up as indicated, then release back to the original note. Only the first note is struck.

**PRE-BEND:** Bend the note as indicated, then strike it.

**VIBRATO:** The string is vibrated by rapidly bending and releasing the note with the fretting hand.

**WIDE VIBRATO:** The pitch is varied to a greater degree by vibrating with the fretting hand.

**HAMMER-ON:** Strike the first (lower) note with one finger, then sound the higher note (on the same string) with another finger by fretting it without picking.

**PULL-OFF:** Place both fingers on the notes to be sounded. Strike the first note and without picking, pull the finger off to sound the second (lower) note.

**LEGATO SLIDE:** Strike the first note and then slide the same fret-hand finger up or down to the second note. The second note is not struck.

**SHIFT SLIDE:** Same as legato slide, except the second note is struck.

**TRILL:** Very rapidly alternate between the notes indicated by continuously hammering on and pulling off.

**TAPPING:** Hammer ("tap") the fret indicated with the pick-hand index or middle finger and pull off to the note fretted by the fret hand.

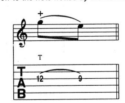

**NATURAL HARMONIC:** Strike the note while the fret-hand lightly touches the string directly over the fret indicated.

**PINCH HARMONIC:** The note is fretted normally and a harmonic is produced by adding the edge of the thumb or the tip of the index finger of the pick hand to the normal pick attack.

**PICK SCRAPE:** The edge of the pick is rubbed down (or up) the string, producing a scratchy sound.

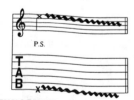

**MUFFLED STRINGS:** A percussive sound is produced by laying the fret hand across the string(s) without depressing, and striking them with the pick hand.

**PALM MUTING:** The note is partially muted by the pick hand lightly touching the string(s) just before the bridge.

**RAKE:** Drag the pick across the strings indicated with a single motion.

**TREMOLO PICKING:** The note is picked as rapidly and continuously as possible.

**VIBRATO BAR DIVE AND RETURN:** The pitch of the note or chord is dropped a specified number of steps (in rhythm) then returned to the original pitch.

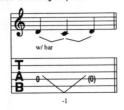

**VIBRATO BAR SCOOP:** Depress the bar just before striking the note, then quickly release the bar.

**VIBRATO BAR DIP:** Strike the note and then immediately drop a specified number of steps, then release back to the original pitch.

# RECORDED VERSIONS
## The Best Note-For-Note Transcriptions Available

RECORDED VERSIONS GUITAR

**ALL BOOKS INCLUDE TABLATURE**

| | | |
|---|---|---|
| 00690016 Will Ackerman Collection .............$19.95 | 00694807 Danny Gatton – 88 Elmira St ..........$19.95 | 00690055 Red Hot Chili Peppers – |
| 00690199 Aerosmith – Nine Lives ...............$19.95 | 00690127 Goo Goo Dolls – A Boy Named Goo ..$19.95 |        Bloodsugarsexmagik ...............$19.95 |
| 00690146 Aerosmith – Toys in the Attic .........$19.95 | 00690338 Goo Goo Dolls – Dizzy Up the Girl ...$19.95 | 00690379 Red Hot Chili Peppers – Californication .$19.95 |
| 00694865 Alice In Chains – Dirt .................$19.95 | 00690117 John Gorka Collection ................$19.95 | 00690090 Red Hot Chili Peppers – One Hot Minute .$22.95 |
| 00694932 Allman Brothers Band – Volume 1 ....$24.95 | 00690114 Buddy Guy Collection Vol. A-J .......$22.95 | 00694892 Guitar Style Of Jerry Reed ............$19.95 |
| 00694933 Allman Brothers Band – Volume 2 ....$24.95 | 00690193 Buddy Guy Collection Vol. L-Y .......$22.95 | 00694937 Jimmy Reed – Master Bluesman .......$19.95 |
| 00694934 Allman Brothers Band – Volume 3 ....$24.95 | 00694798 George Harrison Anthology ...........$19.95 | 00694899 R.E.M. – Automatic For The People ..$19.95 |
| 00694877 Chet Atkins – Guitars For All Seasons ....$19.95 | 00690068 Return Of The Hellecasters ..........$19.95 | 00690260 Jimmie Rodgers Guitar Collection ....$17.95 |
| 00694918 Randy Bachman Collection ...........$22.95 | 00692930 Jimi Hendrix – Are You Experienced? ....$24.95 | 00690014 Rolling Stones – Exile On Main Street ..$24.95 |
| 00694880 Beatles – Abbey Road ................$19.95 | 00692931 Jimi Hendrix – Axis: Bold As Love ...$22.95 | 00690186 Rolling Stones – Rock & Roll Circus ..$19.95 |
| 00694863 Beatles – | 00692932 Jimi Hendrix – Electric Ladyland ....$24.95 | 00690135 Otis Rush Collection ................$19.95 |
|        Sgt. Pepper's Lonely Hearts Club Band ..$19.95 | 00690218 Jimi Hendrix – First Rays of the New Rising Sun $24.95 | 00690031 Santana's Greatest Hits .............$19.95 |
| 00690383 Beatles – Yellow Submarine ..........$19.95 | 00690038 Gary Hoey – Best Of ................$19.95 | 00694805 Scorpions – Crazy World ...........$19.95 |
| 00690174 Beck – Mellow Gold .................$17.95 | 00660029 Buddy Holly .......................$19.95 | 00690150 Son Seals – Bad Axe Blues ..........$17.95 |
| 00690346 Beck – Mutations ...................$19.95 | 00660169 John Lee Hooker – A Blues Legend ..$19.95 | 00690128 Seven Mary Three – American Standards .$19.95 |
| 00690175 Beck – Odelay .....................$17.95 | 00690054 Hootie & The Blowfish – | 00690076 Sex Pistols – Never Mind The Bollocks .$19.95 |
| 00694884 The Best of George Benson ...........$19.95 |        Cracked Rear View ...............$19.95 | 00120105 Kenny Wayne Shepherd – Ledbetter Heights $19.95 |
| 00692385 Chuck Berry .......................$19.95 | 00694905 Howlin' Wolf ......................$19.95 | 00120123 Kenny Wayne Shepherd – Trouble Is ..$19.95 |
| 00692200 Black Sabbath – | 00690136 Indigo Girls – 1200 Curfews ........$22.95 | 00690196 Silverchair – Freak Show ...........$19.95 |
|        We Sold Our Soul For Rock 'N' Roll ....$19.95 | 00694938 Elmore James – | 00690130 Silverchair – Frogstomp ............$19.95 |
| 00690115 Blind Melon – Soup .................$19.95 |        Master Electric Slide Guitar .........$19.95 | 00690041 Smithereens – Best Of .............$19.95 |
| 00690305 Blink 182 – Dude Ranch .............$19.95 | 00690167 Skip James Blues Guitar Collection ..$16.95 | 00694885 Spin Doctors – Pocket Full Of Kryptonite .$19.95 |
| 00690028 Blue Oyster Cult – Cult Classics ......$19.95 | 00694833 Billy Joel For Guitar ...............$19.95 | 00690124 Sponge – Rotting Pinata ............$19.95 |
| 00690219 Blur .............................$19.95 | 00694912 Eric Johnson – Ah Via Musicom .....$19.95 | 00694921 Steppenwolf, The Best Of ...........$22.95 |
| 00694935 Boston: Double Shot Of ..............$22.95 | 00690169 Eric Johnson – Venus Isle ..........$22.95 | 00694957 Rod Stewart – Acoustic Live ........$22.95 |
| 00690237 Meredith Brooks – Blurring the Edges ..$19.95 | 00694799 Robert Johnson – At The Crossroads ....$19.95 | 00690021 Sting – Fields Of Gold .............$19.95 |
| 00690168 Roy Buchanon Collection ............$19.95 | 00693185 Judas Priest – Vintage Hits .........$19.95 | 00690242 Suede – Coming Up ...............$19.95 |
| 00690364 Cake – Songbook ...................$19.95 | 00690277 Best of Kansas .....................$19.95 | 00694824 Best Of James Taylor .............$16.95 |
| 00690337 Jerry Cantrell – Boggy Depot .........$19.95 | 00690073 B. B. King – 1950-1957 ............$24.95 | 00690238 Third Eye Blind ...................$19.95 |
| 00690293 Best of Steven Curtis Chapman .......$19.95 | 00690098 B. B. King – 1958-1967 ............$24.95 | 00690267 311 ..............................$19.95 |
| 00690043 Cheap Trick – Best Of ...............$19.95 | 00690134 Freddie King Collection ............$17.95 | 00690030 Toad The Wet Sprocket ............$19.95 |
| 00690171 Chicago – Definitive Guitar Collection ..$22.95 | 00694903 The Best Of Kiss ..................$24.95 | 00690228 Tonic – Lemon Parade ............$19.95 |
| 00690393 Eric Clapton – Selections from Blues ..$19.95 | 00690157 Kiss – Alive .......................$19.95 | 00690295 Tool – Aenima ....................$19.95 |
| 00660139 Eric Clapton – Journeyman ...........$19.95 | 00690163 Mark Knopfler/Chet Atkins – Neck and Neck $19.95 | 00699191 The Best of U2 – 1980-1990 .......$19.95 |
| 00694869 Eric Clapton – Live Acoustic .........$19.95 | 00690296 Patty Larkin Songbook .............$17.95 | 00694411 U2 – The Joshua Tree .............$19.95 |
| 00694896 John Mayall/Eric Clapton – Bluesbreakers $19.95 | 00690070 Live – Throwing Copper ............$19.95 | 00690039 Steve Vai – Alien Love Secrets ......$24.95 |
| 00690162 Best of the Clash ...................$19.95 | 00690018 Living Colour – Best Of ............$19.95 | 00690172 Steve Vai – Fire Garden ............$24.95 |
| 00690166 Albert Collins – The Alligator Years ...$16.95 | 00694845 Yngwie Malmsteen – Fire And Ice ...$19.95 | 00690023 Jimmie Vaughan – Strange Pleasures ..$19.95 |
| 00694940 Counting Crows – August & Everything After $19.95 | 00694956 Bob Marley – Legend ..............$19.95 | 00690370 Stevie Ray Vaughan and Double Trouble – |
| 00690197 Counting Crows – Recovering the Satellites ..$19.95 | 00690283 Best of Sarah McLachlan ...........$19.95 |        The Real Deal: Greatest Hits Volume 2 ..$22.95 |
| 00690118 Cranberries – The Best of .............$19.95 | 00690382 Sarah McLachlan – Mirrorball .......$19.95 | 00660136 Stevie Ray Vaughan – In Step .......$19.95 |
| 00690215 Music of Robert Cray ...............$19.95 | 00690354 Sarah McLachlan – Surfacing .......$19.95 | 00694835 Stevie Ray Vaughan – The Sky Is Crying .$19.95 |
| 00694840 Cream – Disraeli Gears ..............$19.95 | 00690239 Matchbox 20 – Yourself or Someone Like You $19.95 | 00694776 Vaughan Brothers – Family Style ....$19.95 |
| 00690352 Creed – My Own Pirson ..............$19.95 | 00690244 Megadeath – Cryptic Writings .......$19.95 | 00690217 Verve Pipe, The – Villains ..........$19.95 |
| 00690007 Danzig 4 ..........................$19.95 | 00690236 Mighty Mighty Bosstones – Let's Face It ..$19.95 | 00120026 Joe Walsh – Look What I Did... ....$24.95 |
| 00690184 dc Talk – Jesus Freak ...............$19.95 | 00690040 Steve Miller Band Greatest Hits .....$19.95 | 00694789 Muddy Waters – Deep Blues .......$24.95 |
| 00690333 dc Talk – Supernatural ..............$19.95 | 00694802 Gary Moore – Still Got The Blues ...$19.95 | 00690071 Weezer ...........................$19.95 |
| 00660186 Alex De Grassi Guitar Collection ......$19.95 | 00694958 Mountain, Best Of .................$19.95 | 00690286 Weezer – Pinkerton ...............$19.95 |
| 00690289 Best of Deep Purple .................$17.95 | 00694913 Nirvana – In Utero ................$19.95 | 00694970 Who, The – Definitive Collection A-E ..$24.95 |
| 00694831 Derek And The Dominos – | 00694883 Nirvana – Nevermind ..............$19.95 | 00694971 Who, The – Definitive Collection F-Li ..$24.95 |
|        Layla & Other Assorted Love Songs ....$19.95 | 00690026 Nirvana – Acoustic In New York .....$19.95 | 00694972 Who, The – Definitive Collection Lo-R ..$24.95 |
| 00690322 Ani Di Franco – Little Plastic Castle ...$19.95 | 00690121 Oasis – (What's The Story) Morning Glory $19.95 | 00694973 Who, The – Definitive Collection S-Y ..$24.95 |
| 00690187 Dire Straits – Brothers In Arms .......$19.95 | 00690290 Offspring, The – The Ignition .......$19.95 | 00690320 Best of Dar Williams ..............$17.95 |
| 00690191 Dire Straits – Money For Nothing .....$24.95 | 00690204 Offspring, The – Ixnay on the Hombre ..$17.95 | 00690319 Best of Stevie Wonder .............$19.95 |
| 00695382 The Very Best of Dire Straits – | 00690203 Offspring, The – Smash .............$17.95 | 00690319 Stevie Wonder – Some of the Best ...$19.95 |
|        Sultans of Swing ..................$19.95 | 00694830 Ozzy Osbourne – No More Tears ....$19.95 | |
| 00660178 Willie Dixon – Master Blues Composer ..$24.95 | 00694855 Pearl Jam – Ten ...................$19.95 | |
| 00690250 Best of Duane Eddy .................$16.95 | 00690053 Liz Phair – Whip Smart ............$19.95 | |
| 00690349 Eve 6 .............................$19.95 | 00690176 Phish – Billy Breathes .............$22.95 | |
| 00690323 Fastball – All the Pain Money Can Buy ..$19.95 | 00690331 Phish – The Story of Ghost ..........$19.95 | |
| 00690089 Foo Fighters .......................$19.95 | 00693800 Pink Floyd – Early Classics .........$19.95 | |
| 00690235 Foo Fighters – The Colour and the Shape ..$19.95 | 00694967 Police – Message In A Box Boxed Set ..$70.00 | |
| 00690394 Foo Fighters – | 00694974 Queen – A Night At The Opera ......$19.95 | |
|        There Is Nothing Left to Lose ......$19.95 | 00690395 Rage Against The Machine – | |
| 00694920 Free – Best Of .....................$18.95 |        The Battle of Los Angeles .........$19.95 | |
| 00690324 Fuel – Sunburn ....................$19.95 | 00690145 Rage Against The Machine – Evil Empire ..$19.95 | |
| 00690222 G3 Live – Satriani, Vai, Johnson ......$22.95 | 00690179 Rancid – And Out Come the Wolves ...$22.95 | |